Hunters Helping Hunters is an organization developed to assist families that have had an interruption in the family structure or support. Founded by fellow hunters and outdoorsmen from across the country, Hunters Helping Hunters will assist families who are associated with hunting with their medical or funeral costs due to a family member's death or medical situation. The assistance will help offset the family's financial burden caused by the cost of such an interruption.

Through contributions, donations and other financial aids, Hunters Helping Hunters' goal is for the assistance provided to help alleviate some of the financial issues during these critical times, thus allowing the family to focus more on rebuilding the family structure and support system.

Deer Camp Dan's Cookbook

Deer Camp Dan's Cookbook

Compiled by
Andrea Van Steenhouse
Jean Marie Martini

Simpler Life Press
Denver, Colorado

Published by Simpler Life Press
1599 South Uinta Way
Denver, Colorado 80231

Compiled by Andrea Van Steenhouse & Jean Marie Martini
Cover illustration and illuminations by Johanna Parker
Edited by Michelle Asakawa

Printed in Canada

VanSteenhouse, Andrea
DeerCampDan's Cookbook

p. cm.
Library of Congress Control Number: 2003091538

ISBN 0-9619806-3-X
1 3 5 7 9 10 8 6 4 2
First Edition

To Gordy

Without him and his dream,
HHH and this book would not exist.

Any cookbook is only as good as the recipes in it.
All any author can do is collect those recipes from
friends, foes and family, from near and far, and hope
he has done the best he can to present them in a
useful and entertaining format.

I would like to thank all
who have contributed to make this
dream a reality.

Danny

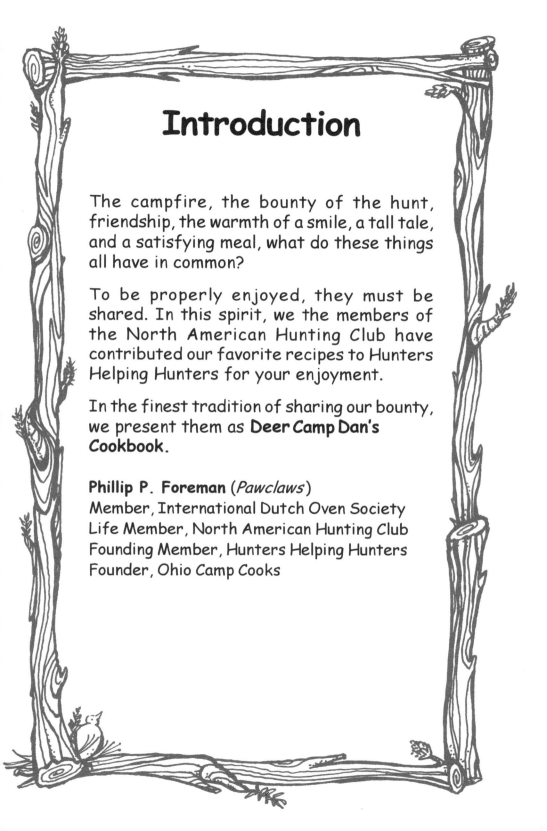

Introduction

The campfire, the bounty of the hunt, friendship, the warmth of a smile, a tall tale, and a satisfying meal, what do these things all have in common?

To be properly enjoyed, they must be shared. In this spirit, we the members of the North American Hunting Club have contributed our favorite recipes to Hunters Helping Hunters for your enjoyment.

In the finest tradition of sharing our bounty, we present them as **Deer Camp Dan's Cookbook**.

Phillip P. Foreman (*Pawclaws*)
Member, International Dutch Oven Society
Life Member, North American Hunting Club
Founding Member, Hunters Helping Hunters
Founder, Ohio Camp Cooks

CONTENTS

The North American Hunting Club proudly presents this special edition cookbook that includes the personal favorites of your fellow members. Each recipe has been screened by a cooking professional and edited for clarity. However, we are not able to kitchen test these recipes and cannot guarantee their outcome or your safety in their preparation or consumption. Please be advised that any recipes that require the use of dangerous equipment (*such as pressure cookers*) or potentially unsafe procedures (*such as marinating, canning, or pickling*) should be used with caution and safe, healthy practices.

STARTERS

FRIED RATTLESNAKE

1 large rattlesnake
1 qt   water
4 T   salt
marinade of choice
1 C   flour
$\frac{1}{8}$ t   paprika
a dash of tarragon
a dash of thyme
olive oil
salt and pepper to taste

1. Mix water and salt in pot. Soak rattlesnake carcass for 2 hours in salt water.
2. Rinse and dry meat well.
3. Cut meat into chunks to fry.
4. Marinate meat for 6-7 hours.
5. Mix together flour, paprika, tarragon and thyme, and pepper to taste. Dredge meat in this.
6. Heat olive oil. Fry chunks of prepared rattler in oil until golden brown. Drain on paper towels and serve hot.

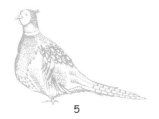

ELK JERKY

2 lbs   elk, sliced thinly
½ t   seasoned salt
½ t   garlic powder
½ t   black pepper
¼ t   cayenne pepper
1 t   onion powder
1 t   liquid smoke
¼ C   Worcestershire sauce
¼ C   soy sauce

1. Combine everything, mixing well.

2. Let marinate at least overnight in the refrigerator.

3. Dry in dehydrator until leathery, about 4-6 hours, depending on the thickness of the meat.

Tip: The meat is much easier to slice when it is partially frozen.

VENISON JERKY

dehydrator
4 lbs venison
3 C soy sauce
8 oz brown sugar
4 T crushed red pepper, divided
4 oz liquid smoke

1. Thaw venison, then put back in freezer for 2 hours. This hardens the meat enough to slice it easily. Do not refreeze.

2. Slice it into $\frac{3}{16}$" to $\frac{1}{4}$" thick strips. Remove all fat and silver skin from the sliced meat.

3. Combine all ingredients except venison and 2 T crushed pepper in large bowl (*approximately 5 qts*). Mix well.

4. Marinate the venison about 15-20 minutes, then lay out on racks in dehydrator.

5. Sprinkle remainder of pepper on if you like it hot or add any other seasoning you may prefer. Set your dehydrator to the manufacturer's recommendation for cooking your meat.

GRILLED RATTLESNAKE WITH SALSA CUBANO

1 lb   rattlesnake meat
$\frac{2}{3}$ C   olive oil
6-8   cloves garlic, minced
$1\frac{1}{2}$ C   fresh orange juice or lime juice
1 t   ground cumin
salt and freshly ground black pepper, to taste

1. Cut meat into 4" strips.
2. Mix together remaining ingredients. Marinate and refrigerate the rattlesnake in 1 cup of the Salsa Cubano for at least 4-6 hours.
3. Remove from marinade and grill strips for 2 minutes on each side.
4. Brush reserved cup of marinade on meat and serve.

Makes 2 cups

NICK'S NUTZ

1 C   soy sauce
1 T   garlic, chopped
2 oz   Jack Daniels®
2   large red onions, Stockton Flats
6-10   testes from mature buck deer

1. Cut testes into $\frac{1}{4}$" slices.

2. Mix soy sauce with chopped garlic and liquor in mixing bowl.
   Add testes. Cover and set in refrigerator or cooler.

3. Slice red onions in skillet and sauté until softened.
   Add the marinated testes to the skillet and bring to simmer.

4. Let cook for 10 minutes or until desired consistency is
   obtained.

**This recipe is best used after the harvest of a number of
bucks!**

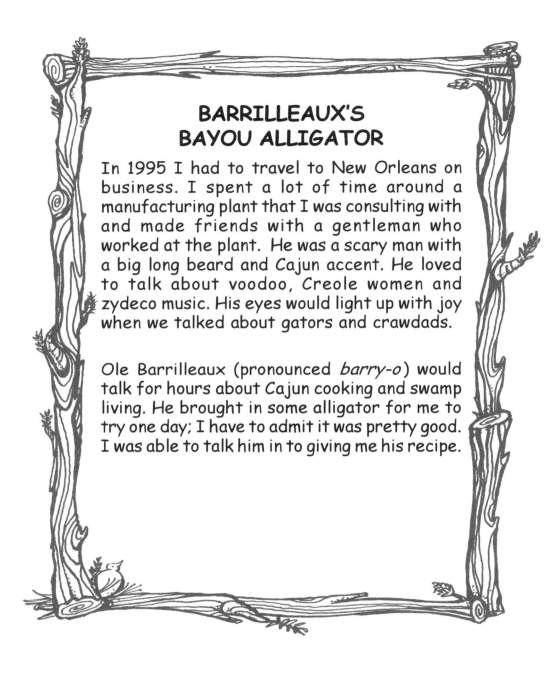

BARRILLEAUX'S BAYOU ALLIGATOR

In 1995 I had to travel to New Orleans on business. I spent a lot of time around a manufacturing plant that I was consulting with and made friends with a gentleman who worked at the plant. He was a scary man with a big long beard and Cajun accent. He loved to talk about voodoo, Creole women and zydeco music. His eyes would light up with joy when we talked about gators and crawdads.

Ole Barrilleaux (pronounced *barry-o*) would talk for hours about Cajun cooking and swamp living. He brought in some alligator for me to try one day; I have to admit it was pretty good. I was able to talk him in to giving me his recipe.

BARRILLEAUX'S BAYOU ALLIGATOR STRIPS

1 lb alligator tail, cut into 2-3" strips.
$\frac{1}{4}$ C chopped onions
$\frac{1}{4}$ C chopped green onions
$\frac{1}{4}$ C chopped celery
$\frac{1}{4}$ C chopped green bell peppers
$1\frac{1}{2}$ T minced fresh garlic
2 T fresh basil, chopped
2 t fresh oregano
1 bay leaf
$2\frac{1}{2}$ C peeled and chopped tomatoes
3 C chicken broth (*canned stock will work*)
$\frac{1}{2}$ T cayenne pepper
salt and black pepper to taste
2 T butter
2 T chopped green onions
2 C cooked white rice
3 T olive oil

1. Heat the olive oil in a cast-iron skillet.
   (*Ole Barrilleaux demanded that the skillet be cast iron*).
   Then sear the alligator meat.

2. Add the onions and green onions, celery, bell peppers and
   garlic. Sauté for 2-3 minutes or until veggies start to wilt.
   Add the basil, oregano and bay leaf. Sauté for another
   minute. Add the tomatoes and chicken broth.

3. Season with cayenne, salt and pepper to taste.

4. Simmer the sauce until gator meat is tender. Add the butter
   as needed. Top with remaining green onions and serve with
   cooked rice.

Serves 4-6

MARIAN'S SWEET POTATO DIP

18-oz package light cream cheese
2 C sweet potatoes, mashed
1½ T jalapeno peppers, minced
1 t Worcestershire sauce
1 t Louisiana Hot Sauce®
1 t Lawry's® seasoned salt
¼ C minced onion
¼ C finely chopped pecans
1 t garlic salt
1 t onion

1. Let cream cheese come to room temperature.

2. Boil sweet potatoes in jackets until tender.
   Peel, mash and cool.

3. Blend sweet potatoes and cream cheese.
   Add remaining ingredients and mix thoroughly.

4. Shape in small balls and serve on crackers or make a large ball.

Best if made early in the day or kept in container overnight.

SAUSAGE & CHEESE SNACKS

2 lbs   pork or venison sausage, uncooked
1½ C   biscuit mix
16 oz   cheddar cheese, grated, or 4 C, shredded
½ C   finely chopped onions
½ C   finely chopped celery
½ t   garlic powder

1. Mix all ingredients well and form into 1" balls.

2. Place on ungreased cookie sheet.

3. Bake at 375 degrees for 15 minutes or until golden brown.

These can be made ahead of time and frozen uncooked.
Just take out of freezer, thaw and bake as above.

Makes 6 dozen

STUFFED MUSHROOMS

1 lb mushrooms, cleaned of any dirt
1 lb   crab meat
¼ C   finely chopped onion
¼ C   finely chopped celery
2 T   mayonnaise
½ C   breadcrumbs
½ C   cheese—mozzarella or provolone, finely grated
1 t   Old Bay® seasoning
dash or 2 of Tabasco®
cherry tomatoes
bacon

1. Remove stems from mushrooms; chop stems fine.
2. Add ½ cup stems to remaining ingredients and mix well.
3. Fill mushroom caps with crab mixture about ¾"–1" above cap.
4. Top with cherry tomato and wrap with a strip of bacon around crab mixture above mushroom cap.
5. Bake at 350 degrees until bacon is crisp. Serve warm.

Serves 4

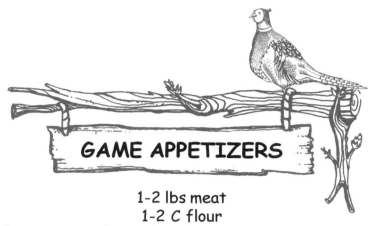

GAME APPETIZERS

1-2 lbs meat
1-2 C flour
½-1 C seasoned breadcrumbs or crackers, crushed
3-6 T lemon pepper
½-1 t salt
corn oil for frying

1. Prepare meat, removing any silver skin and everything else except red meat. Wash well. Pat meat dry.
2. Mix together remaining ingredients except oil.
3. Coat meat with batter mixture and deep fry in hot corn oil until done.

SPICY MEATBALLS

1 lb ground venison, antelope,
moose, bear, etc.
1   can cranberry sauce
1   jar hot salsa

1. Make meatballs out of ground meat.
2. Place on cookie sheet and bake in 350 degree oven for 25 minutes to precook and remove excess oils.
3. Place precooked meatballs in crockpot and add cranberry sauce and hot salsa. Cook on low heat all day.

Can be served on sandwich rolls or as appetizers.

Serves 4

CRAB CAKES

1 lb crab meat
¼ C green pepper, finely chopped
¼ C onion, finely chopped
¼ C mayonnaise
1 large egg
½-¾ C Italian seasoned breadcrumbs
1 T Old Bay seasoning®
½ t dry mustard
dash of Worcestershire sauce
dash of red pepper sauce

1. Combine all ingredients in a large bowl, using just enough breadcrumbs to hold cakes together.
2. Make into patties and fry in melted shortening until golden brown on each side.

Serves 2-4

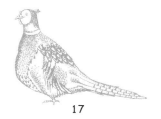

RATTLESNAKE CREAM CHEESE MIX

1 lb   bell peppers, diced $\frac{1}{4}$"
1 lb   yellow onions, diced $\frac{1}{4}$"
$\frac{1}{4}$ C   butter
$3\frac{1}{2}$ lb   cream cheese
1 C   sour cream
2 T   Old Bay® seasoning
2   dried chipotle peppers
2 T   lemon juice
$\frac{1}{2}$ T   Worcestershire sauce
$\frac{1}{2}$ lb   cooked rattlesnake meat

1. Sauté peppers and onions in butter until onions become translucent, and then place in refrigerator to cool down.
2. Place remaining ingredients in mixing bowl; add cool pepper and onion mixture. Mix at low speed until well blended.
3. Run on high speed for 1 minute.
4. Scoop cream into a dish and add cooked rattlesnake meat to top.

Serve hot with tortilla chips and lime wedges.

Makes 1$\frac{1}{2}$ quarts
Cesar Garcia
Buckhorn Exchange

CHILE RELLENOS

pancake batter
sliced green chilies
sliced cheese

1. Put a tablespoon of pancake batter on hot greased griddle.
2. Lay a slice of green chilies and a half slice of cheese on top of the batter.
3. Top with another tablespoon of batter, then flip over and cook until golden brown. Repeat with remaining batter.

Similar to chile rellenos without the mess and fuss.

GOOSE
HORS D'OEUVRES

1 goose, boned
1 bottle Italian salad dressing
¼ t lavender, finely diced
flour
cooking oil

1. Slice goose ½" thick.

2. Marinate in salad dressing and lavender for 3-4 hours.

3. Drain.

4. Coat with flour.

5. Fry in hot cooking oil for 3-4 minutes per side, or until done.

6. Cut into bite-sized pieces and serve.

PICO DE GALLO

2 medium tomatoes, chopped
8 jalapeno peppers, seeded and chopped
1 white onion, peeled and chopped
3 cloves garlic, peeled and minced
$\frac{1}{2}$ C fresh lemon (*or lime*) juice
1 C fresh cilantro, chopped
(*I don't always add this much—*
too much cilantro tastes like dishwashing liquid!)
salt and freshly ground black pepper to taste

1. In a bowl, combine all the ingredients except salt and pepper. Stir together well.
2. Season to taste with salt and pepper. Serve with tortilla chips or as a side relish with poultry, venison, beef, or whatever.

You may want to double or quadruple the quantity—people tend to be disappointed when you run out!

A variation: Add chunks of three or four ripe avocados for a wonderful guacamole condiment; just cut back a bit on the lemon/lime juice so it won't be soupy.

Serves 4

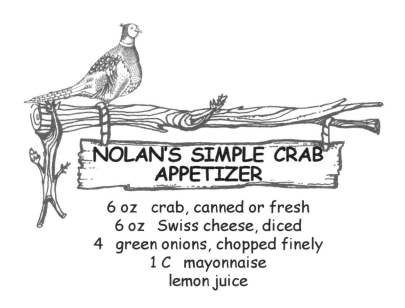

NOLAN'S SIMPLE CRAB APPETIZER

6 oz   crab, canned or fresh
6 oz   Swiss cheese, diced
4   green onions, chopped finely
1 C   mayonnaise
lemon juice

1. Mix all ingredients together.
2. Bake at 350 degrees for 30 minutes
3. Serve with crackers or chips

Serves 4

BREADS

CAMP FIRE CAST IRON BREAKFAST

6   slices of bacon
2   tomatoes, diced
½ C sharp cheddar cheese, grated
6   eggs, beaten
1 T   chives, chopped
1 T   parsley, chopped
1 T   Worcestershire sauce
salt and pepper

1. Cook bacon until crisp and drain on paper towel, leaving fat in skillet.

2. Add tomatoes to bacon fat and sauté 3 minutes.

3. Blend in cheese.

4. Pour eggs into skillet and cook mixture on low heat, turning it gently until eggs are set but soft.

5. Chop bacon into small pieces and add to egg mixture. Add herbs and seasonings.

Serves 2

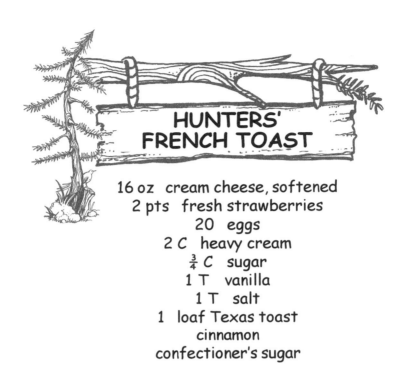

HUNTERS' FRENCH TOAST

16 oz cream cheese, softened
2 pts fresh strawberries
20 eggs
2 C heavy cream
$\frac{3}{4}$ C sugar
1 T vanilla
1 T salt
1 loaf Texas toast
cinnamon
confectioner's sugar

1. Mix cream cheese and strawberries. Set aside.

2. Whisk eggs, cream, sugar, vanilla and salt.

3. Dip bread slices into egg mixture and place one layer deep in well-greased 9" x 13" baking dish.

4. Spread with cream cheese mixture. Repeat bread layer.

5. Sprinkle with cinnamon, and confectioner's sugar.

6. Cover with foil and bake at 375 degrees for 30 minutes or until firm.

Serves 8

DUCK BLIND
BREAKFAST BURRITO

1 T   butter or margarine
3 T   onion, finely chopped
3 T   green pepper, finely chopped
8   eggs
¼ C   milk
½ C   salsa
1 C   Monterey jack cheese, grated
4   large flour tortillas

1. Melt butter in cast iron skillet.

2. Saute onions and pepper.

3. Beat eggs and milk together and add to pan.

4. Cook until fluffy. Add salsa and cheese and cook until cheese melts.

5. Serve in warmed flour tortillas.

Serves 4

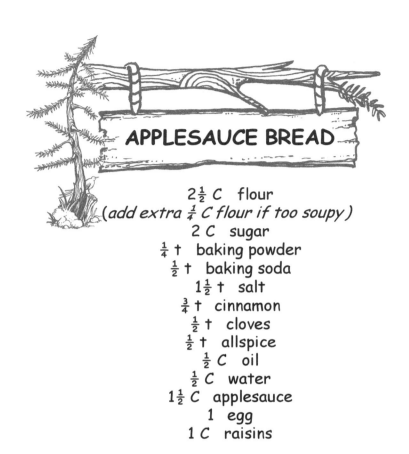

APPLESAUCE BREAD

2½ C flour
(*add extra ¼ C flour if too soupy*)
2 C sugar
¼ t baking powder
½ t baking soda
1½ t salt
¾ t cinnamon
½ t cloves
½ t allspice
½ C oil
½ C water
1½ C applesauce
1 egg
1 C raisins

1. Combine all ingredients together and mix well.
2. Place mixture into 2 well-greased 5 x 9" loaf pans.
3. Bake at 350 degrees for 50 minutes.

Makes 20–24 servings

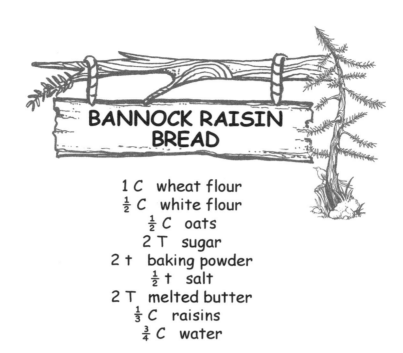

BANNOCK RAISIN BREAD

1 C   wheat flour
½ C   white flour
½ C   oats
2 T   sugar
2 t   baking powder
½ t   salt
2 T   melted butter
⅓ C   raisins
¾ C   water

1. Stir together wheat and white flour, oats, sugar, baking powder and salt.
2. Add melted butter, raisins and water, adding more water if needed to make a fairly wet dough.
3. With floured hands, pat into greased 9" pie plate.
4. Bake in 400-degree oven for 20 to 25 minutes.

Serves 4

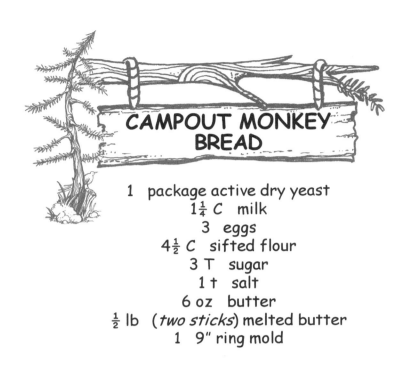

CAMPOUT MONKEY BREAD

1 package active dry yeast
1¼ C milk
3 eggs
4½ C sifted flour
3 T sugar
1 t salt
6 oz butter
½ lb (*two sticks*) melted butter
1 9" ring mold

1. Mix yeast with small amount of the milk until dissolved, according to package. Add 2 eggs and beat.

2. Mix in dry ingredients. Add remaining milk a little at a time, mixing thoroughly.

3. Cut in butter until well blended. Knead dough until satiny. Cover and let rise in a warm area 1 to 1½ hours or until doubled in size.

4. Butter and flour the ring mold. Roll out dough onto a lightly floured board; shape into a log.

5. Cut into 24 pieces of equal size. Shape each piece of dough into a ball; roll in melted butter. Place 12 balls in the bottom of the mold, leaving space between. Place remaining balls on top, spacing evenly. Let dough rise in mold for 30 minutes.

6. Beat the last egg with about a teaspoon of water and brush tops of dough.

7. Bake in preheated Dutch oven at 375 degrees until golden brown, 25-30 minutes. Remove from heat, cool slightly, and remove from mold.

Note: *Make sure your Dutch oven is large enough to hold the ring mold. If not, disregard the instructions concerning the mold; grease the oven liberally with butter-flavored vegetable shortening and follow the remaining directions.*

DOUGHNUTS WITH SWEET MILK

3 eggs, well beaten
1 C sugar
1 C milk
$3\frac{1}{2}$ C sifted flour
4 t baking powder
1 t salt
$\frac{1}{2}$ t nutmeg
1 t vanilla extract
3 T butter, melted
oil or fat for frying

1. Beat eggs using rotary whisk. Beat in sugar. Stir in milk. Add sifted dry ingredients, vanilla extract and melted butter. (*This dough is soft, but the doughnuts are light.*)

2. Toss one third of dough on floured board. Knead lightly. Roll to $\frac{1}{4}$" thickness. Use floured board knife to prevent sticking. Use floured cutter.

3. Fry 4 or 5 doughnuts at a time in deep hot fat 2-3 minutes. Turn often. Drain on brown paper.

To render the fat, you can use a crockpot on a low-temp setting until melted.

Makes about 1 dozen

DIANNE'S CORIANDER HONEY BREAD

2 pkgs   yeast
½ C   warm water
¼ t   ground ginger
½ t   sugar
2   eggs
¾ C   honey
1½ T   ground coriander
1 t   cinnamon
½ t   ground cloves
1½ t   salt
½ C   melted butter
1½ C   warm milk
7 C   flour, approximately

DIANNE'S CORIANDER HONEY BREAD con't

1. In small bowl combine yeast, water, ginger and $\frac{1}{2}$ t sugar. Stir with fork until dissolved. Set aside.

2. In large bowl, whisk until smooth eggs, honey, coriander, cinnamon, cloves and salt. Blend in yeast mixture, melted butter and milk.

3. Beat in 3 cups of flour until smooth. Gradually add flour, small portions at a time, until a soft, workable dough is formed. Be careful when adding flour because the dough can easily become dry.

4. Turn out on a lightly floured board and knead until smooth and elastic, about 10 minutes.

5. If dough remains sticky, rub soft butter on hands and continue kneading.

6. Place in a warm, greased bowl turning to coat the top; cover loosely with plastic wrap and towel.

7. Allow to double in bulk, about 2-2$\frac{1}{2}$ hours.

8. Punch down and turn out onto floured surface. Knead lightly, cover and let rest 10 minutes.

9. Shape loaves, place in greased pans, cover and let double about 1$\frac{1}{2}$ hours, or until just curved over tops of pans.

10. Bake in preheated 300-degree oven for 45 minutes for $8\frac{1}{2} \times 4\frac{1}{2} \times 2\frac{1}{2}$" loaf pans.

11. Loosen sides with a spatula and carefully turn out on wire racks to cool.

Makes 3 loaves

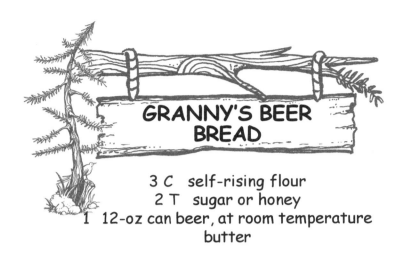

GRANNY'S BEER BREAD

3 C   self-rising flour
2 T   sugar or honey
1   12-oz can beer, at room temperature
butter

1. Combine flour, sugar or honey and beer and mix 14 strokes.
2. Put into buttered loaf pan and let rise 15 minutes.
3. Bake at 350 degrees for 1 hour 10 minutes.
4. Butter top when it comes out of oven.

Can also use 1½ cups of stale beer from keg at room temperature instead of can.

Makes 1 loaf

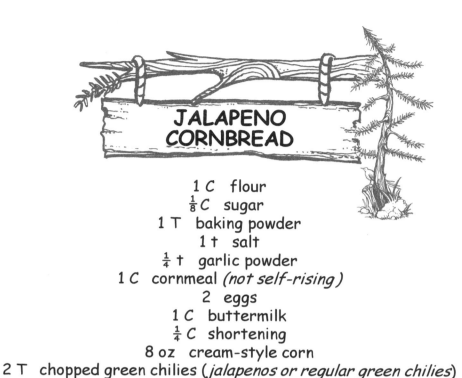

JALAPENO CORNBREAD

1 C   flour
$\frac{1}{8}$ C   sugar
1 T   baking powder
1 t   salt
$\frac{1}{4}$ t   garlic powder
1 C   cornmeal *(not self-rising)*
2   eggs
1 C   buttermilk
$\frac{1}{4}$ C   shortening
8 oz   cream-style corn
2 T   chopped green chilies (*jalapenos or regular green chilies*)

1. Combine first 6 ingredients in a medium-size mixing bowl.

2. Add eggs, buttermilk and shortening to flour-cornmeal mixture and beat until smooth. Add corn and chopped chilies and blend well.

3. Pour mixture into a greased and floured 8"-square baking pan. Bake in preheated oven at 425 degrees for 35-40 minutes, or until cornbread is golden brown.

4. Cut into squares and serve.

May be frozen. Goes great with chili, pinto beans, or just about any wild game dish.

Yields 16 one-inch squares

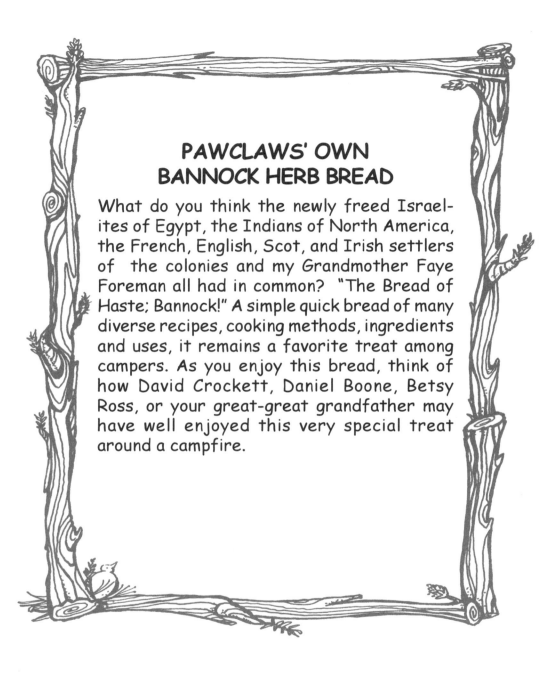

PAWCLAWS' OWN
BANNOCK HERB BREAD

What do you think the newly freed Israel-ites of Egypt, the Indians of North America, the French, English, Scot, and Irish settlers of the colonies and my Grandmother Faye Foreman all had in common? "The Bread of Haste; Bannock!" A simple quick bread of many diverse recipes, cooking methods, ingredients and uses, it remains a favorite treat among campers. As you enjoy this bread, think of how David Crockett, Daniel Boone, Betsy Ross, or your great-great grandfather may have well enjoyed this very special treat around a campfire.

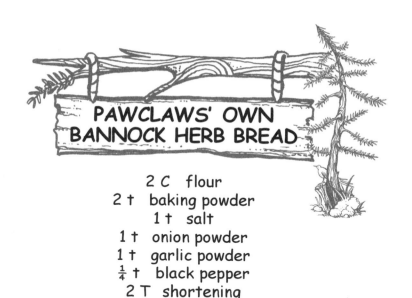

PAWCLAWS' OWN
BANNOCK HERB BREAD

2 C   flour
2 t   baking powder
1 t   salt
1 t   onion powder
1 t   garlic powder
¼ t   black pepper
2 T   shortening
1½ C   water

1. Combine all dry ingredients. Add the shortening and work into a crumbled, cornmeal-like mixture.

2. Add the water and combine until completely absorbed.
   You will probably need to add more water. Add and stir in additional water until you achieve a consistency similar to cornbread or thick plaster. A spoon should be able to easily stand up when inserted into the mix.

3. The batter may be fried on the stove as "spoon bread," dropped into hot grease in serving-size portions, rolled into a snake and wrapped around a stick and baked over the campfire, or baked in a very hot 400-425 degree oven for 15 to 20 minutes. For oven baking, pour the batter into a well-greased 9" pan.

The end result is a golden brown bread. If baked on a campfire don't forget to rotate the stick every few minutes. When fried, turn once when the edges are dry and bubbles break the surface.

Serves 2

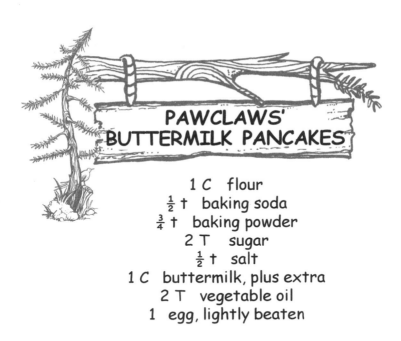

PAWCLAWS' BUTTERMILK PANCAKES

1 C flour
½ t baking soda
¾ t baking powder
2 T sugar
½ t salt
1 C buttermilk, plus extra
2 T vegetable oil
1 egg, lightly beaten

1. Combine dry ingredients.
2. In a separate container combine the wet ingredients.
3. Heat a heavy nonstick skillet or griddle (*a well-seasoned cast-iron skillet may be used*) over medium-high heat to 375 degrees. When hot, lightly brush surface with oil.
4. Combine all ingredients and mix until well combined.
5. Additional buttermilk may be added if the mix appears too thick. Do not overmix. The batter does not need to be creamy or totally smooth.
6. Place about ⅓ cup of batter per pancake in skillet and cook 2-3 minutes, or until small holes appear in batter and the edges begin to dry. Turn cakes and cook about 1 minute until browned.
7. Put cakes in a 200-degree oven until ready to serve.

Serves 4

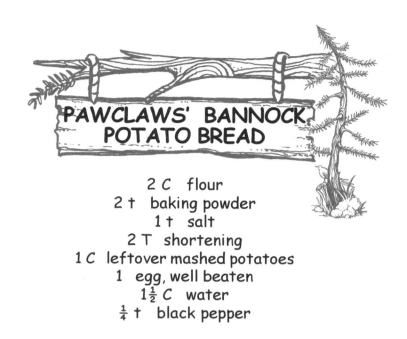

PAWCLAWS' BANNOCK POTATO BREAD

2 C   flour
2 t   baking powder
1 t   salt
2 T   shortening
1 C   leftover mashed potatoes
1   egg, well beaten
1½ C   water
¼ t   black pepper

1. Combine flour, baking powder and salt.

2. Add the shortening and work into a crumbled, cornmeal-like mixture. Combine the mashed potatoes with the dry ingredients and add the egg. Mix well. Add the water and combine until completely absorbed. You will probably need to add more water. Add and stir in additional water until you achieve a consistency similar to cornbread batter or thick plaster. A spoon should be able to easily stand up when inserted into the batter.

3. The mixture may be fried on the stove as "spoon bread," dropped into hot grease in serving-size portions, rolled into a snake and wrapped around a stick and baked over the campfire, or baked in a very hot 400-425 degree oven for 15 to 20 minutes.

4. For oven baking pour the batter into a well-greased 9" square pan. The end result is a golden brown bread. If baked on a campfire don't forget to rotate the stick every few minutes. When fried, turn once when the edges are dry and bubbles break the surface.

Serves 3-4

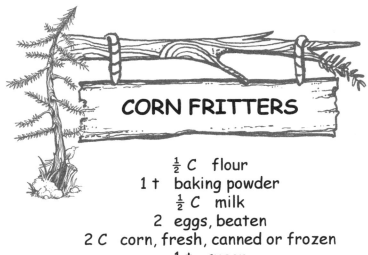

CORN FRITTERS

½ C flour
1 t baking powder
½ C milk
2 eggs, beaten
2 C corn, fresh, canned or frozen
1 t sugar
¼ t salt
¼ t pepper
oil for frying

1. Make a batter with flour, baking powder and milk.
2. Mix in eggs, corn, sugar, salt and pepper.
3. In frying pan heat about ¼ inch of oil over medium-high heat.
4. Drop fritter mixture with spoon into hot oil; brown on both sides. Drain. Repeat for all batter.

Makes about a dozen

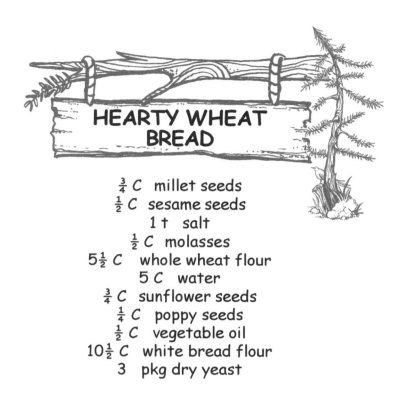

HEARTY WHEAT BREAD

$\frac{3}{4}$ C millet seeds
$\frac{1}{2}$ C sesame seeds
1 t salt
$\frac{1}{2}$ C molasses
$5\frac{1}{2}$ C whole wheat flour
5 C water
$\frac{3}{4}$ C sunflower seeds
$\frac{1}{4}$ C poppy seeds
$\frac{1}{2}$ C vegetable oil
$10\frac{1}{2}$ C white bread flour
3 pkg dry yeast

1. Soften yeast in 100-degree cup warm water.

2. Combine water, molasses, oil and salt.

3. Stir in whole-wheat flour, seeds and part of white bread flour, beating well.

4. Add enough flour to be moderately stiff.

5. Knead 10 – 12 minutes

6. Cover in greased bowl until doubled.

7. Punch and divide, shape and cover, let rise again.

8. Bake at 300 degrees for 45 minutes or until top is brown and sounds hollow when tapped.

Makes 4 loaves

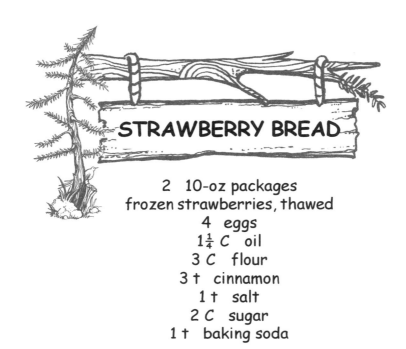

STRAWBERRY BREAD

2 10-oz packages
frozen strawberries, thawed
4 eggs
$1\frac{1}{4}$ C oil
3 C   flour
3 t   cinnamon
1 t   salt
2 C   sugar
1 t   baking soda

1. Beat strawberries, eggs and oil together.
2. Stir in remaining ingredients until well blended.
3. Pour into two loaf pans.
4. Bake at 350 degrees for 45–60 minutes until toothpick comes out clean.

MEXICAN SPOON BREAD

1 lg can   Grands® Buttermilk Biscuits
1 sm can   Grands® Buttermilk Biscuits
16-oz jar   chunky salsa
1 lb   Jimmy Dean® sage sausage, cooked & drained
2 C   Monterey jack and cheddar cheese, grated

1. Cut biscuits into eights.
2. Pour salsa over them and mix.
3. Fold cooked sausage in mixture and put into greased baking pan.
4. Sprinkle cheese over top and cook at 350 degrees for 30-45 minutes.

Serves 4

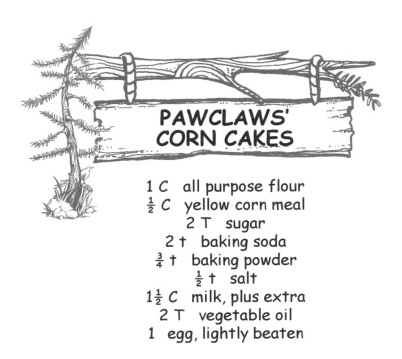

PAWCLAWS' CORN CAKES

1 C   all purpose flour
½ C   yellow corn meal
2 T   sugar
2 t   baking soda
¾ t   baking powder
½ t   salt
1½ C   milk, plus extra
2 T   vegetable oil
1   egg, lightly beaten

1. Combine dry ingredients.

2. In a separate container combine the wet ingredients.

3. Heat a heavy nonstick skillet or griddle (*a well-seasoned cast iron skillet may be used*) over medium high heat to 375 degrees. When hot, lightly brush surface with oil.

4. Combine the ingredients until well mixed. Additional milk may be added if the mix appears too thick. Do not over mix. The batter does not need to be creamy or smooth.

5. Place about ⅓ cup batter per pancake in skillet and cook 2-3 minutes, or until small holes appear in batter and the edges begin to dry. Turn cakes and cook about 1 minute or until browned. Serve immediately or keep warm in a 200 degrees oven until ready to serve.

Serves 6

BREAKFAST CORNBREAD SOUFFLE

2¾ C   milk
⅔ C   corn meal
1¾ T   butter
¾ t   salt
3   eggs, separated

1. Sift corn meal into almost boiling milk; stir constantly until thick.
2. Beat and cool. Beat in egg yolks one at a time.
3. Add stiffly beaten egg whites.
4. Bake at 375 degrees for 40 minutes. Serve immediately.

Serves 4

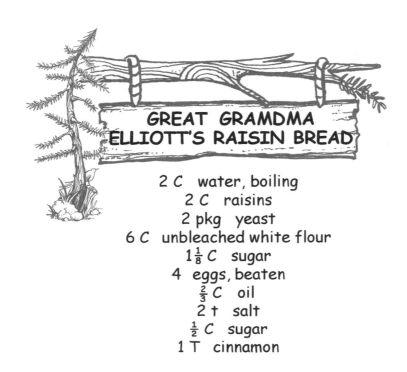

GREAT GRAMDMA ELLIOTT'S RAISIN BREAD

2 C   water, boiling
2 C   raisins
2 pkg   yeast
6 C   unbleached white flour
$1\frac{1}{8}$ C   sugar
4   eggs, beaten
$\frac{2}{3}$ C   oil
2 t   salt
$\frac{1}{2}$ C   sugar
1 T   cinnamon

1. Boil raisins & let sit for 5 minutes. Drain and reserve liquid.

2. Sift flour into large glass bowl. Make a well in center.

3. Dissolve yeast in $\frac{1}{2}$ C warm raisin water. Pour this into flour well.

4. Sprinkle 1 T sugar over yeast. Cover, let rise 30 minutes. Mixture should be bubbly.

5. Add eggs, oil, salt and remaining sugar. Mix with spoon. Mixture should still be warm.

6. Add remaining warm raisin water and the raisins. Knead until smooth and elastic, adding more flour if necessary.

7. Let rise at least $1\frac{1}{2}$ hours until double. Punch down, cover with damp cloth and let rise again until double. Punch down.

8. Divide into thirds and roll out to approximately 9" x 6". Sprinkle with cinnamon sugar. Let rise again in greased pans.

9. Bake at 350 degrees for 15 minutes then 325 degrees for 25 minutes.

MARINADES

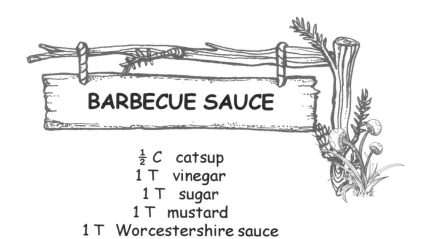

BARBECUE SAUCE

½ C   catsup
1 T   vinegar
1 T   sugar
1 T   mustard
1 T   Worcestershire sauce

Mix all ingredients well.

Can be used as a quick BBQ sauce on the grill or over an open fire.

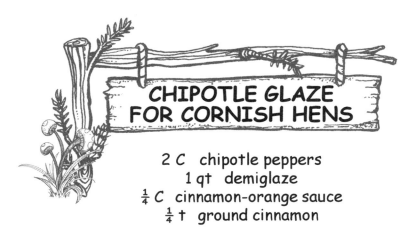

CHIPOTLE GLAZE FOR CORNISH HENS

2 C   chipotle peppers
1 qt   demiglaze
¼ C   cinnamon-orange sauce
¼ t   ground cinnamon

1. Puree chipotle peppers.
2. Combine all ingredients in a saucepan. Cook until thickened.
3. Remove from heat. Store refrigerated or frozen, using as needed to glaze broiled or roasted Cornish hens.

Cesar Garcia
Buckhorn Exchange

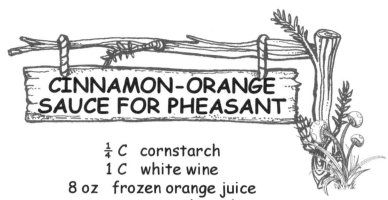

CINNAMON-ORANGE SAUCE FOR PHEASANT

$\frac{1}{4}$ C   cornstarch
1 C   white wine
8 oz   frozen orange juice concentrate, thawed
1 qt   water
2 lbs   orange marmalade
1 t   ground cinnamon
$\frac{1}{4}$ C   brown sugar
4 t   chicken base

1. Combine cornstarch and wine in a small bowl.
2. Combine remaining ingredients in a saucepan.
3. Bring to a boil, then add cornstarch and wine combination.
4. Return to boil. Lower heat and allow to simmer for 5 minutes.

Serve hot over pheasant breast.

Makes 2 qts

Cesar Garcia
Buckhorn Exchange

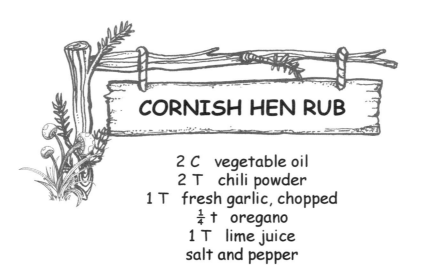

CORNISH HEN RUB

2 C   vegetable oil
2 T   chili powder
1 T   fresh garlic, chopped
¼ t   oregano
1 T   lime juice
salt and pepper

1. Combine all ingredients.
2. Rub Cornish hens with mixture.
   Marinate overnight for better flavor.

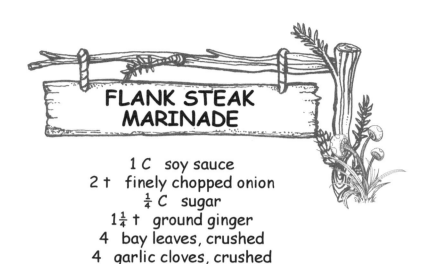

FLANK STEAK MARINADE

1 C soy sauce
2 t finely chopped onion
$\frac{1}{4}$ C sugar
$1\frac{1}{4}$ t ground ginger
4 bay leaves, crushed
4 garlic cloves, crushed

1. Combine all ingredients in a large ziplock bag.

2. Add flank steak to bag and allow to marinate at least 2 hours.

3. Grill 20 minutes per side.

GINGER MARINADE

$\frac{3}{4}$ C   dry white wine
3 T   vegetable oil
2 T   soy sauce
3 T   minced onion
2   garlic cloves, minced
1 t   minced fresh gingerroot
1$\frac{1}{2}$ t   salt
1 T   toasted sesame seeds

Combine all ingredients.

Makes about 1 cup

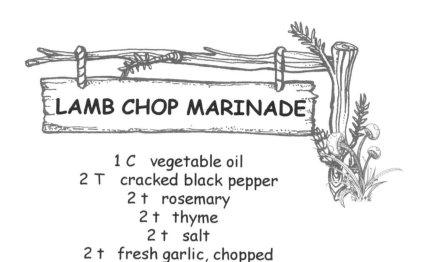

LAMB CHOP MARINADE

1 C   vegetable oil
2 T   cracked black pepper
2 t   rosemary
2 t   thyme
2 t   salt
2 t   fresh garlic, chopped

1. Combine all ingredients.
2. Rub on lamb chops and marinate overnight.

Makes 1 cup

Cesar Garcia
Buckhorn Exchange

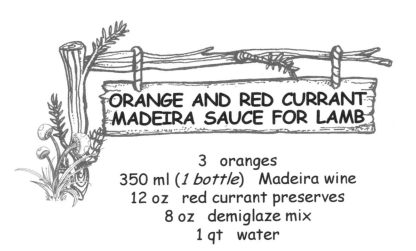

ORANGE AND RED CURRANT MADEIRA SAUCE FOR LAMB

3 oranges
350 ml (*1 bottle*) Madeira wine
12 oz red currant preserves
8 oz demiglaze mix
1 qt water

1. Remove all zest from oranges; combine zest with wine and preserves in small saucepan.
   (*Use the oranges for another purpose.*)
2. Place on stove and reduce by half.
3. Combine demiglaze with reduction. Bring to boil and simmer for 5 minutes.

Serve warm over grilled or roasted lamb.

Cesar Garcia
Buckhorn Exchange

ORANGE MARINADE FOR FISH

¼ C   orange juice
2 T   soy sauce
2 T   catsup
2 T   salad oil
2 T   parsley, chopped
1 T   lemon juice
1   garlic clove, minced
1 T   brown sugar
½ t   salt
1 T   toasted sesame seeds
fish steaks or fillets

1. Combine all ingredients except sesame seeds.
   Place fish in glass baking dish in one layer.
2. Pour marinade over fish and allow to stand for 30 minutes.
   Turn once.
3. Place fish on grill and cook 10 minutes per 1" thickness,
   basting with reserved marinade. Turn fish halfway through
   cooking.
4. Sprinkle sesame seeds on cooked fish. Serve.

Makes about ½ C marinade, enough for 2

PRICKLY PEAR APRICOT SAUCE FOR QUAIL

1 C   gin
¾ T   grated fresh gingerroot
1 qt   prickly pear puree
1 C   apricot puree
20 oz   cranberry juice
¼ C   cornstarch
¼ C   cold water

1. Combine gin and ginger in a medium saucepan, bring to boil and add the two purees.
2. In small bowl combine cornstarch and water.
3. Return gin mixture to boil, then add cornstarch and water mixture; simmer for 5 minutes.

Makes about 2 qts

Cesar Garcia
Buckhorn Exchange

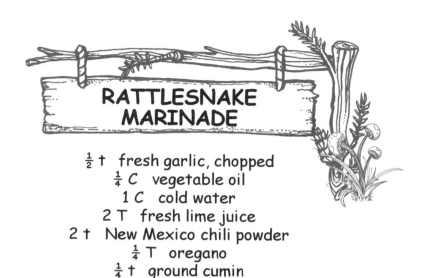

RATTLESNAKE MARINADE

$\frac{1}{2}$ t fresh garlic, chopped
$\frac{1}{4}$ C vegetable oil
1 C cold water
2 T fresh lime juice
2 t New Mexico chili powder
$\frac{1}{4}$ T oregano
$\frac{1}{4}$ t ground cumin

1. Combine all ingredients; add rattlesnake and marinate, not longer than 1 hour.
2. Cook rattlesnake until tender.

Makes about 1$\frac{1}{2}$ cups

Cesar Garcia
Buckhorn Exchange

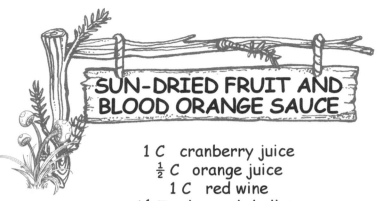

SUN-DRIED FRUIT AND BLOOD ORANGE SAUCE

1 C   cranberry juice
½ C   orange juice
1 C   red wine
1½ T chopped shallots
1 T   juniper berries
1 T   cracked black pepper
1 T   chicken base
8 oz   dried fruit—cherries, cranberries, currants, blueberries
¼ C   cold water
¼ C   cornstarch

1. In saucepan, mix all ingredients except water and cornstarch. Mix water and cornstarch in small bowl.
2. Bring saucepan ingredients to a boil, and then add water and cornstarch mix. Let simmer for 5 minutes on low heat.

Serve over venison.

Makes 1 qt

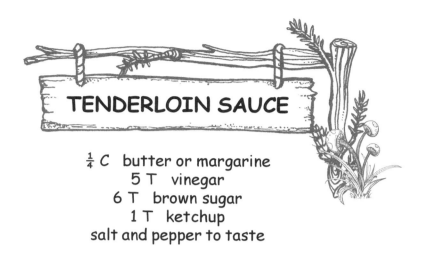

TENDERLOIN SAUCE

$\frac{1}{4}$ C   butter or margarine
5 T   vinegar
6 T   brown sugar
1 T   ketchup
salt and pepper to taste

1. Heat all ingredients to boiling.
2. If mixture separates, reheat.

Works well on any meat.
Tastes even better after refrigerated for next day's leftovers.

Makes about $\frac{1}{2}$ C

CHICKEN MARINADE

Italian dressing
barbeque powder
oregano
garlic powder

1. Mix together dressing and barbecue powder.
   Add oregano mixed with garlic powder to make a thick sauce.
2. Brush it on chicken as you are cooking the chicken.

Good with any type of chicken, especially when done on grill or open fire.

MAIN COURSES

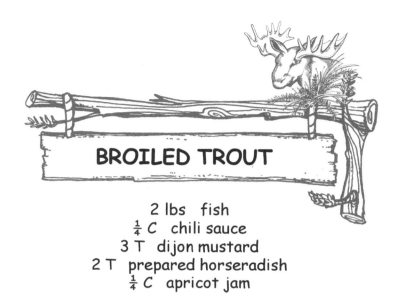

BROILED TROUT

2 lbs   fish
$\frac{1}{4}$ C   chili sauce
3 T   dijon mustard
2 T   prepared horseradish
$\frac{1}{4}$ C   apricot jam

1. Wash fish.

2. Mix together remaining ingredients.

3. Brush mixture on fish.

4. Grease grill and broil about 5 minutes per side or until done.

Serves 2-4

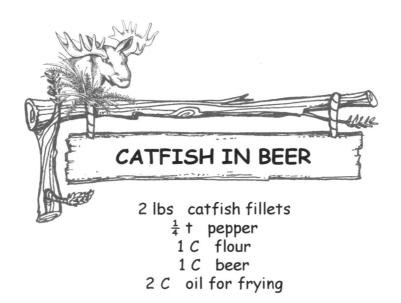

CATFISH IN BEER

2 lbs catfish fillets
$\frac{1}{4}$ t   pepper
1 C   flour
1 C   beer
2 C   oil for frying

1. Wash and dry catfish.
2. Mix pepper with flour and add beer gradually to make a smooth batter.
3. Heat oil for frying.
4. Cover fillets in batter.
5. Fry fillets about 4 minutes each, until golden brown.

Serves 2-4

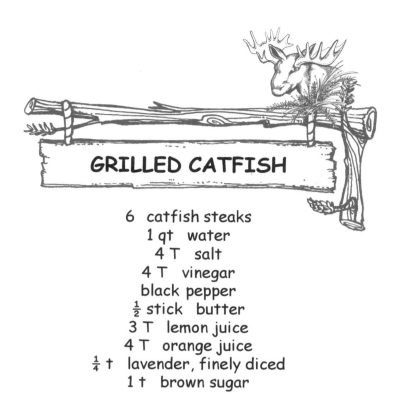

GRILLED CATFISH

6 catfish steaks
1 qt water
4 T salt
4 T vinegar
black pepper
½ stick butter
3 T lemon juice
4 T orange juice
¼ t lavender, finely diced
1 t brown sugar

1. Soak catfish at least 2 hours in 1 quart water, salt and vinegar.

2. Pepper steaks to taste.

3. Combine butter, lemon juice, orange juice, lavender and brown sugar in small saucepan and heat until butter melts.

4. Place steaks on grill about 8" from the flame and baste often with sauce. Grill until brown, about 10 minutes per side.

Serves 4-6

BROILED RED SNAPPER

6   red snapper steaks
         salt
       pepper
      paprika
$\frac{1}{4}$ stick butter
4 T   lemon juice
1 t   brown sugar
$\frac{1}{3}$ C   white wine

1. Sprinkle salt, pepper and paprika on steaks.

2. In saucepan, combine remaining ingredients.
   Heat until butter melts.

3. Brush steaks with sauce.

4. Broil 8" from flame, basting often.
   Cook about 10 minutes per side, until fish flakes when poked
   with a fork

Serves 4-6

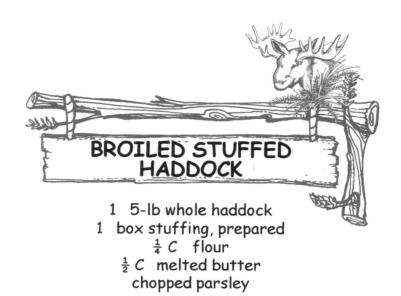

BROILED STUFFED HADDOCK

1　5-lb whole haddock
1　box stuffing, prepared
$\frac{1}{4}$ C　flour
$\frac{1}{2}$ C　melted butter
chopped parsley

1. Clean and scale whole fish.

2. Stuff fish with stuffing.

3. Dust with flour and brush with melted butter.

4. Broil under low heat for 15 minutes per side, brushing with butter, until done.

5. Serve with parsley.

Tip: When scaling fish, rub fish with vinegar and scales will remove more easily.

Serves 2-4

SALMON STEAKS

6   salmon steaks
3 T   prepared mustard
¼ C   butter
½ C   apple cider

1. Clean salmon.

2. Spread salmon with mustard.

3. Melt butter in skillet and add cider.

4. Sauté salmon for 10 minutes on each side or until done.

Serves 6

SMOKED MULLET

1-1½ lbs   mullet
BBQ sauce
lemon juice
salt and pepper

1. Clean out the innards and cut off heads.
2. Cut the fish from the bottom, laying it open like a butterfly.
   Sprinkle with lemon, salt and pepper to taste.
3. Brush on thin layer of BBQ sauce.
4. Place in smoker at about 175 degrees and smoke for
   1 to 2 hours, or until meat is flaky but not dry.
   Baste with sauce while smoking.

Serve with coleslaw and garlic bread. Also works with mackerel and kings.

Serves 2

BAKED GOOSE

2   boneless goose breasts
1 t   salt
1 t   pepper
2   eggs, beaten
1 C   cracker crumbs
1   stick butter
1 C   orange juice
$\frac{3}{4}$ C   tomato juice
$\frac{1}{2}$ C   white wine
1   clove garlic, finely chopped
2   bay leaves
$\frac{1}{2}$ C   sour cream

1. Season goose breasts with salt and pepper.
   Dip in egg, then roll in cracker crumbs.

2. Brown breasts in butter over medium heat.

3. Place in baking dish.

4. Combine all remaining ingredients except sour cream.
   Pour over breasts in pan.

5. Cover and bake at 250 degrees for 3 hours. Remove bay
   leaves. Gently stir sour cream into the sauce just before
   serving.

Serves 2

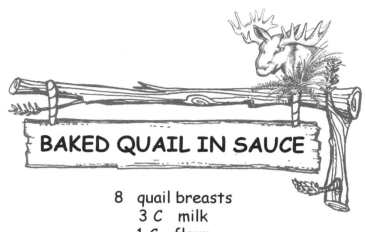

BAKED QUAIL IN SAUCE

8   quail breasts
3 C   milk
1 C   flour
1   stick butter
1   onion, finely chopped
1   green pepper, finely chopped
1   can condensed cream of chicken soup
¼ C   sherry wine
½ C   milk
salt and pepper to taste

1. Soak quail breasts overnight in 3 C milk.

2. Roll soaked breasts in flour.

3. Quickly brown in butter over medium heat.

4. Place breasts in baking dish.

5. Save ½ of the drippings.

6. Sauté onion and pepper in drippings.

7. Add soup, wine, remaining milk, salt and pepper to pan and pour over quail.

8. Cover and bake at 300 degrees for 45 minutes.

Serves 4-6

73

PHEASANT SURPRISE

2 pheasant breasts
3 T butter
2 T shallots, finely diced
1 C brandy
2 C chicken broth
$\frac{1}{3}$ C prepared horseradish
1 C heavy cream

1. Split each pheasant breast in two.
2. Using an ovensafe skillet, sauté breasts in butter and shallots until brown.
3. Add brandy to the drippings. Carefully light the brandy. When the brandy burns down, pour two cups of chicken broth into the skillet.
4. Bake at 350 degrees for 1 hour.
5. Mix together the horseradish and cream and add to the pan; bake an additional 15 minutes.

Serve with wild rice.

Serves 2

DEEP FRIED PHEASANT

pheasant
injectable Creole, butter and garlic marinade
Oklahoma Joe's Hog Rub and Yard Bird Seasoning®
peanut oil for frying

1. Pluck your bird and clean out the entrails. Wash the bird thoroughly with cold water and dry with paper towels.
2. With a marinade injector, inject Creole, butter and garlic marinade into the breast, thighs and legs.
3. Rub the entire bird inside and out with Oklahoma Joe's Hog Rub and Yard Bird Seasoning. Let stand for 1 hour.
4. Preheat peanut oil in a turkey or fish cooker to 375 degrees. Use enough oil to barely cover the birds and cook for $3\frac{1}{2}$ minutes per pound. Same recipe can be used for wild turkey.

Serves 4

DOVES a la VIN

8-10   dove breasts
6 T   flour
salt and pepper to taste
$\frac{1}{4}$ t   ground ginger
$\frac{3}{4}$ C   olive oil
3   cloves garlic
1$\frac{1}{2}$ C   each red wine and water

1. Combine flour, salt, pepper and ginger.
2. Wet doves and coat in flour mixture.
3. Heat oil with garlic cloves. Brown doves.
4. Add wine and water. Cover and simmer until tender,
   1$\frac{1}{2}$-2 hours.
5. Add leftover flour mixture to thicken gravy.

Serve with rice.

Serves 4-6

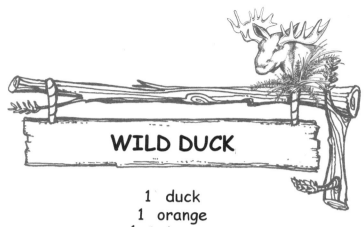

WILD DUCK

1 duck
1 orange
½ C butter
3 T finely diced onion
2 T finely chopped parsley
2 T finely diced orange rind

1. Wash duck.
2. Stuff cavity of duck with whole unpeeled orange.
3. Roast in oven at 300 degrees for about 45 minutes.
4. To make orange sauce, brown onion in butter.
   Add remaining ingredients.
5. Simmer and serve.

Serve with rice.

Serves 3-4

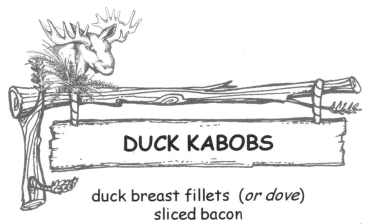

DUCK KABOBS

duck breast fillets (*or dove*)
sliced bacon
pearl onions or 1 large onion, cut into approx. $1\frac{1}{2}$" × $1\frac{1}{2}$" pieces
green peppers, cut into $1\frac{1}{2}$" × $1\frac{1}{2}$" pieces
pineapple chunks, canned or fresh
whole mushrooms (*optional*)
barbecue sauce

1. Soak fillets in salt water overnight, then cut into pieces about $1\frac{1}{2}$" square. For doves, just remove fillets from breastbone in halves.

2. Wrap each piece in $\frac{1}{2}$ slice of bacon.

3. Alternate putting meat and vegetable pieces on skewers, making sure to start and finish with meat as this helps to hold the vegetables on the skewer.

4. Barbecue over medium heat, basting with barbecue sauce frequently.

4. Turn often and cook until meat is done, usually 15-20 minutes, or when bacon is starting to burn around the edges.

Serve over rice.

DUCK WITH LAVENDER

2 ducks
1 T butter
3 T lemon juice
$\frac{1}{8}$ t lavender, finely diced
$\frac{1}{4}$ t salt and pepper to taste
8 strips bacon
$\frac{1}{2}$ C butter, melted

1. Clean and split ducks.
2. Mix 1 T butter with 1 T lemon juice and lavender. Rub over duck.
3. Add salt and pepper to taste.
4. Wrap each half in 2 strips of bacon.
5. Broil ducks about 10 minutes on each side, basting frequently with melted butter and remaining 2 T of lemon juice.

Serves 4-6

HOT CHICKEN SALAD

4 C cooked chicken, chunked
2 C celery, chopped and cooked
4 hard-boiled eggs, chopped
1 can cream of chicken soup
1 can cream of mushroom soup
1 T onion, chopped
1 C white American cheese, grated
1 stick butter, melted
8 slices bread, cubed

1. Mix first 6 ingredients and put in large casserole dish.

2. Top with cheese.

3. Mix melted butter with cubed bread; put on top of cheese.

4. Cover dish with foil.

5. Bake at 400 degrees for 30 minutes.

6. Remove foil for last 10-15 minutes

Serves 4-6

MOTHER HUBBARD'S WHITE LIGHTNIN'

1 lb   boneless,
skinless chicken breasts, cubed
1   medium onion
1½ t   garlic powder
1 T   vegetable oil
2   15-oz cans great northern beans, drained and rinsed
1   14½-oz can chicken broth
2   4-oz cans chopped green chilies
1 t   salt
1 t   ground cumin
1 t   dried oregano
½ t   black pepper
¼ t   cayenne pepper
1 C   sour cream
½ C   whipping cream

1. Sauté chicken, onion and garlic until the chicken is no longer pink.
2. Add beans, broth, chilies and seasonings. Bring to a boil.
3. Reduce heat and simmer 30 minutes.
4. Stir in sour cream and whipping cream and serve immediately.

Serves 4

HOBO CHICKEN

game bird
marinade or injection sauce
peanut oil
butter
vegetables such as carrots, peas, onions, green pepper
seasonings

At home:

1. Take one whole, dressed game bird and prep with your favorite marinade or injection sauce prior to the trip.

At camp:

2. Place bird on piece of tin foil that is large enough to wrap entire bird.
3. Brush bird on outside with peanut oil. If you soaked the bird in marinade instead of injecting it, rub foil with a bit of butter to cut down on sticking.
4. Stuff body cavity with your favorite vegetables and seasonings.
5. Wrap the package so that the only opening is at the end of the drumsticks. This will be the upside.
6. Let the fire die down a little and pull back coals to make room for the package.
7. Place package in and gently pull coals back around it all the way to the top, leaving just a little exposed for the next step.
8. After you have the coals situated, unroll the opening a little or punch some small holes in the upside so the pressure from the steam can escape and not cause a rupture under the coals.
9. Size of the bird dictates cooking time. A 4-lb chicken cooks in about $2\frac{1}{2}$ hours.

Makes 1 bird, enough for 3-4 servings

WILD TURKEY BAKE

2 small turkeys
4 T honey
salt and pepper
$\frac{1}{2}$ stick butter, melted
$\frac{1}{2}$ C chopped onion
1 C chicken stock
1 C white wine
1 t chopped parsley

1. Cut each turkey into four pieces. Brush with honey.

2. Add salt and pepper to taste.

3. Place in baking dish and bake 30 minutes at 450 degrees. Baste often with melted butter.

4. Mix onion, chicken stock, wine and parsley and pour over turkey pieces.

5. Reduce heat to 250 degrees.
   Cover and bake approximately 1 hour.

Serves 6

DADDY CHICKEN

You will need a smoker pit, charcoal, and mesquite
blocks for this recipe.

medium-size chicken
1   Red Delicious apple, diced
1   red onion, diced
1   can mushrooms
7   shakes Worcestershire sauce
red wine
garlic salt
6   shakes Tony Chacheres Original Spice®
3   shakes oregano
4   caps Mr. Yoshida's Ginger Garlic Teriyaki Sauce®
1 C   water
1   16-oz pkg Chef Williams Cajun Injectable Marinade
Creole Butter Recipe® (*8-10 oz per bird*)
1   bag charcoal
1   bag mesquite blocks (*not chips*)

DADDY CHICKEN con't

1. Clean the bird. Tastes best if you get bird prepared 4 hours prior to cooking.
2. Use $\frac{1}{2}$ apple per bird, $\frac{1}{2}$ red onion per bird, and $\frac{1}{2}$ can mushrooms per bird.
3. Mix all ingredients except chicken, Creole Recipe, and water by hand in a bowl. Use lots of garlic salt. Set aside.
4. Inject $\frac{1}{6}$ cup of water each into left breast, the right breast, left leg, right leg and then turn bird over and inject it in the thigh in the back on the left and on the right side. You'll see the water under the skins and it makes the skin rise. (*Get it into the bird, not just under the skin.*)
5. Take 8-10 oz. Creole Recipe per bird and do the exact same thing. Don't be surprised if you see marinade and water coming out of the holes. That means you are doing a good job.
6. Stuff the cavity of the bird with the apple mixture. Fasten shut or leave it open.
7. Place chicken in the smoker pit, using charcoal and mesquite blocks. Cook at 250 degrees for four hours.

The bird is done when you can take the leg and bend it back and it breaks freely from the body. If the legs are tight, it is not done. The longer you cook it, however, the dryer the breast gets.

Keep the mesquite on the coals to have constant flow of smoke. Temperature should never get below 200 degrees or above 300. 250 degrees is ideal.

GAME BIRDS IN
BROCCOLI CREAM SAUCE

2 lbs   chicken breasts or large game bird skinned and boned
(*about four portions*)
1 C   broccoli florets, washed and trimmed
3 T   olive oil
salt and pepper to taste
2 T   butter
1   lemon
1 C   heavy cream
a pinch of MSG (*optional*)

1. Place the broccoli in a saucepan and cover with water.
   Bring to a boil over high heat.

2. Reduce heat and continue to simmer for about 10 minutes, until
   broccoli is tender.

3. Meanwhile, in a large sauté pan over medium-high heat, add the
   olive oil and quickly brown the breasts. After browning both
   sides, season the breasts with a little salt and pepper, reduce the
   heat to medium-low and cover.

4. Remove the broccoli to a cutting board and finely dice;
   return to the original pot. Season the broccoli to taste with the
   salt and pepper.

5. Return the broccoli to a simmer and add the butter.
   Slice the lemon in half and add about 1½ t of lemon juice to the
   broccoli. This should be a little less than the juice of
   one-half lemon.

6. Slowly add the cream to the broccoli pot to achieve a fairly thick
   soup (*about the density of a cream of mushroom soup or
   chowder*). Taste the sauce and adjust seasonings as required.
   Add MSG if using.

7. Slice the unused lemon half into thin slices, one for each portion
   of breast. Turn the breasts and place one lemon slice atop each.

8. Pour the broccoli sauce into the pan with the breasts and gently
   combine the sauce and the pan drippings. Reduce the heat to low,
   cover and continue cooking until the breasts are
   thoroughly cooked through.

Serves 4

PAWCLAWS' OWN BOVINE ALFREDO AND NOODLES

1   large sweet onion, thinly sliced
3 T   extra-virgin olive oil
1 lb   lean precooked roast beef, thinly sliced
1   medium tomato, peeled, seeded, and finely diced
1   head garlic, finely diced
salt and pepper to taste
6 oz   fettuccini noodles, prepared according to package
directions and salted with sea salt
10 oz   prepared Alfredo sauce

1. In a large skillet sauté the onion in the olive oil until clear.
2. Add the roast beef, tomato, garlic, and salt and pepper.
   Stir to combine and heat through.
3. Warm the Alfredo sauce in a separate pan.
   Meanwhile prepare the noodles and drain.
4. When the beef has begun to absorb the pan liquids remove
   from heat and plate the dish as follows: Noodles to cover the
   center to the rim of the plate, the Alfredo sauce to thinly
   cover the noodles to within 2" of the outer perimeter of the
   noodles, then the meat sauce in the center, with slices of beef
   neatly arranged.

Serve with a green salad and garlic toast.

Serves 4

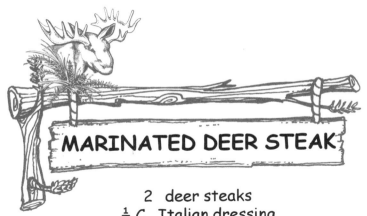

MARINATED DEER STEAK

2 deer steaks
½ C Italian dressing
2 T Dale's® sauce
1 T Worcestershire sauce
2 cloves garlic
2 slices onion (*can substitute onion powder*)
pepper
water
butter

1. In a bowl, mix Italian dressing, Dale's® sauce, garlic, onion slices and pepper. Add steaks. Add water, if needed, until marinade covers sides of steaks. Poke a few holes in each steak to let marinade penetrate.

2. Let stand in refrigerator 6–8 hours.

3. To grill, use very hot fire and sear both sides of steak quickly, then move them to side of grill out of direct flame.

4. Slow cook and baste with butter and sauce.

5. For added flavor, put garlic cloves and onion slices directly on coals to steam flavor into meat.

6. For pan cooking, just slow cook to taste.

Serves 2

BAGGED VENISON ROAST

2 venison steaks, $\frac{1}{4}$" thick
1 Reynolds® oven bag large size
1 T flour
1 T minced onion
1 4-oz can sliced mushrooms
1 16-oz can tomato wedges, drained
1 t salt
$\frac{1}{2}$ t pepper
$\frac{1}{2}$ t allspice

1. Place flour in oven bag. Set bag in roasting pan.
2. Put onion, mushrooms, tomato wedges, salt, pepper and allspice in bag, mixing gently.
3. Add venison.
4. Tie bag shut and make 4 or 5 slits in top.
5. Cook for 15 minutes at 350 degrees.

Serves 2

KINGLY TURKEY
'N' HAM À LA PAWCLAWS

2 T olive oil
¼ C diced carrot
¼ C diced celery
¼ C diced sweet onion
9 T flour, divided
2¼ C milk, divided
1 t baking powder
½ C diced cooked smoked lean ham
¼ C diced cooked turkey breast
¼ t salt
½ t Salt Free 17®
dash fresh black pepper
dash MSG or Accent®

1. Preheat oven to 425 degrees. Heat the olive oil in a saucepan. Add the vegetables to the hot oil and stir-fry about 1 minute. **Do not overcook.**

2. Reduce the heat to low and add 3 T of the flour to form a roux. Add 2 cups of the milk and return the heat to medium. Cook, stirring occasionally, until sauce reaches a full boil.

3. At a boil, add the diced ham and turkey and stir. Reduce the heat to low and heat through.

4. Meanwhile, in a separate bowl, combine the remaining flour, baking powder and a dash of salt. Mix this with about ¼ C milk to form a dough.

5. Add the seasonings to the white sauce and stir through. Remove the pan from the heat and spoon the contents into 4 7-oz ramekins.

6. Separate the biscuit dough into 4 portions. Using hands wet with cold water, form into flat biscuits and place one on top of each ramekin. There is no need to completely cover the top or seal the edges.

7. Place the ramekins in a shallow roasting pan and put the pan in an oven, preheated to 425 degrees. Bake 12 – 15 minutes, or until the biscuits are raised and browned

Note: This dish is easily finished in camp using a Coleman® oven. In a homemade box oven, the dish should be baked with 6 fully active charcoal briquettes for about 12 minutes.

Serves 4

STUFFED ROUND STEAK

1 lg   venison, moose or elk round steak,
1 foot square and 1" thick
salt, pepper, garlic and meat tenderizer to taste
2   large onions, chopped
1   green pepper, chopped
½   stick butter, divided
1 C   mushrooms, sliced
2 C   toasted breadcrumbs
½ C   red wine
2 t   dried oregano
½ C   cream of mushroom soup
minced garlic to taste

1. Sear steak on both sides in a large skillet with butter approximately 8-10 minutes on each side.

2. Remove meat and place flat on aluminum foil.

3. Sauté onions and green pepper in 1 t butter.

4. Add all other ingredients. Mix well.

5. Spread on steak.

6. Roll up and tie with baker's string every 3 inches.

7. Close up foil and bake at 250 degrees for about 3 hours.

8. Melt remaining butter with minced garlic to taste, and baste frequently.

Serves 4

SIMPLY STEAK

back straps from deer
Italian dressing
bacon

1. Take the back straps from your deer and butterfly cut them into filets according to directions below.
2. Take a toothpick and punch several holes through the filet to allow the marinade to penetrate the meat.
3. Place all filets in a sealable container and cover with your favorite Italian dressing.
   (*No cheap fat-free stuff for this—get the good stuff.*)
   Allow the filets to marinate at least 12 hours in the refrigerator/cooler.
4. When you are ready to cook, remove the filets from the container and wrap each one with a strip of bacon. Pin the bacon with a toothpick. This is more to hold them together than season them.
5. Cook over a concentrated heat for 3 minutes on each side.

Serve with your favorite vegetables or baked potato. My favorite side is baked sweet potato, oozing with butter, sugar and cinnamon.

CAUTION: Do not get any juice from this on your face; your tongue will beat you to death trying to get to it.

Directions for butterfly cut:

1. Take the back strap and lay it out sinew-side down.
2. Move in from one end about 1-1½" and cut down to the sinew. Do not cut through the sinew.
3. Move the same distance beyond the cut and cut all the way through.
4. Lay the filet out like an open book so the sinew folds in half.

CHEESY STEAKS

1-2 lbs venison or elk steaks
$3\frac{1}{2}$ C grated cheddar cheese
3 C water, divided
$1\frac{1}{2}$ C milk
1 t garlic powder
$\frac{3}{4}$ C flour
potatoes
2 C chopped onion
salt and pepper

1. Mix 2 cups water with the milk and garlic powder and bring to a boil. Stir to prevent scorching.

2. Mix remaining 1 cup water with the flour to make a thick sauce.

3. Slice enough potatoes, $\frac{1}{8}$" thick, to fill a 10" x 15" x 2" baking dish half full.

4. Mix in the onion and sprinkle with a little salt and pepper. Pour the sauce over top.

5. Slice the meat into steaks $\frac{1}{4}$"-$\frac{1}{2}$" thick. Spread them out on top of the potatoes and sauce.

6. Cover the whole thing with the cheese.

7. Bake at 350 degrees until the potatoes are tender, 1-$1\frac{1}{2}$ hours.

Serves 2-4

DEER STEAKS, MIKE'S WAY

deer steaks
bottle of Lea and Perrin's "Sweet and Spicy" Steak Sauce®
Bisquick All-Purpose Baking Mix®
garlic powder
black pepper
salt (*optional*)
butter

1. Marinate steaks in steak sauce for 1 hour, or at least 20 minutes.

2. Preheat griddle or frying pan to about 350 degrees.

3. Mix garlic powder and black pepper to taste (*and salt, if using*) in Bisquick (*a cup of Bisquick will cover about 3-4 medium steaks*)

4. Melt butter in pan or griddle.

5. Dredge meat in mix until covered completely.

6. Fry in melted butter for 4 minutes each side until golden brown.

Do not over cook—the longer you cook, the tougher it gets. Aim for a white to pink color in the center and golden brown on the outside. If meat starts to darken too fast, add butter to pan and turn down heat.

Serve with white rice and soy sauce or potatoes and veggies, on plain bread with some extra salt and pepper.

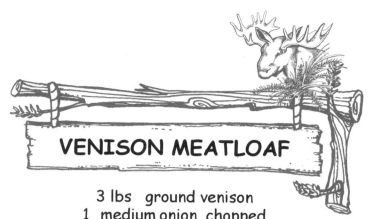

VENISON MEATLOAF

3 lbs   ground venison
1   medium onion, chopped
2   large eggs
$\frac{1}{4}$ C   Worcestershire sauce
$\frac{1}{4}$ C   yellow mustard
$\frac{3}{4}$ C   catsup
1 sleeve saltine crackers, crushed
freshly ground pepper to taste

1. In a large mixing bowl combine all ingredients. Mix thoroughly with hands.
2. Place in 13" X 9" glass pan sprayed with no-stick spray and form into loaf.
3. Bake at 350 degrees for 1 hour or until done through center.

Serves 6-8

JAEGER SCHNITZEL

Sauce:

1–1½ lbs sliced mushrooms
(*morel, chanterelles, meadow mushrooms or*
fairy ring are best for wild mushroom fans)
¾ C chopped green onions
3-4 cloves garlic, chopped
4 T butter
2 T rice vinegar
4 C beef broth
¼ C water
4 T cornstarch
salt

1. Sauté mushrooms, onions and garlic in butter.

2. Add the rice vinegar and beef broth and bring to a boil.

3. Thicken with mixture of cornstarch and water. Add salt to taste.

JAEGER SCHNITZEL con't

Schnitzel:

1 venison back strap cut into $\frac{3}{4}$" butterfly steaks
flour
cornmeal
vegetable oil
butter

1. Using a meat mallet, beat the steaks until they are as thin as possible and still hold together. Roll the steaks in equal amounts of flour and cornmeal. Sauté in hot oil and butter until both sides are golden brown.
2. Ladle sauce over steaks. Serve.

Serve with a baked potato and your favorite side dish.

Serves 6

VENISON AND PORK COMBINATION ROAST

2 T   garlic powder
2 T   onion powder
1 T   ground ginger
1 T   gourmet pepper blend with green, red, white,
and coriander berries
1 T   Salt Free 17®
1 t   black pepper, freshly cracked
2 lbs   venison roast with all fat, sinew and silver skin removed
2 lbs   pork tenderloin roast
8   medium potatoes, peeled
1   large sweet onion, cut into eighths
4   large carrots, peeled and cut into 3" lengths
3 T   cornstarch
2 C   water

1. Combine all seasonings to make a rub. Rub this all over the roasts. Preheat the oven to 325 degrees.

2. Place the seasoned meat into an oven bag prepared according to bag directions and allow to rest and come to room temperature.

3. Surround the meat with the vegetables and seal the bag according to directions. Place the bag into a roasting pan and put pan in oven. Allow to bake for approximately 2 hours. This will provide roasts that are fork-tender and flaking.

4. Remove the roasts from the oven and check with a meat thermometer. A temperature of 180 degrees is desired for well-done roasts. Allow the roasts to rest for 15 minutes before serving.

5. Prepare gravy using the drippings and 3 T cornstarch mixed with 2 C water.

Serves 6

VENISON BURGUNDY

3 lbs   deer meat, cubed
2   cans cream of mushroom soup
1   pkg Lipton® onion soup mix or 1 medium onion,
chopped finely
2   6-oz jars button mushrooms, drained
½ C   burgundy wine
1 C   water

1. Mix all ingredients well in a cast-iron Dutch oven.
2. Bake covered at 350 degrees for 3 hours, taking care to add water as needed. Check often.

Enjoy over a bed of noodles or rice.

Serves 6

VENISON ENCHILADAS

3 oz red wine
½ can of beer
dash of your favorite hot sauce
1 medium onion, diced
3 T olive oil
1-2 garlic cloves, chopped
2 palmfuls chopped cilantro
1 lb ground venison
pinch of coarsely ground black pepper
dash of ground ginger
3 T ground cumin
3 T chili powder
1 12-oz can diced tomatoes
2-3 chopped green chilies, or one small can chilies
½ t chili powder
1 t ground cumin
chopped cilantro
10 medium tortillas
8 oz shredded cheese
1 12-oz can refried beans

VENISON ENCHILADAS con't

1. Mix wine, beer and dash hot sauce with enough water to make 1 C. Set aside.
2. Sauté onion in oil until it begins to turn clear. Add garlic cloves and sauté 30 seconds. Add a palmful of cilantro.
3. Remove a couple spoonfuls of this and set aside.
4. Add ground meat to the remaining sauté a handful at a time mixing until all the meat is blended and browned.
5. Season with the pinch of ground pepper, dash of ginger and 3 T each of cumin and chili powder. Add another palmful of cilantro if desired.
6. Add the liquid mixture to the meat and simmer on low heat for 30 minutes or until liquid is absorbed.
7. For sauce, mix diced tomatoes into the reserved sautéed onions. Heat on medium.
8. Mix in chopped chilies. Add $\frac{1}{2}$ t chili powder and 1 t cumin. Stir occasionally and cook until tomatoes become pasty.
9. Mix in a little chopped cilantro and remove from heat.
10. To make enchiladas, lightly fry or heat tortillas.
11. Fill tortillas with meat filling, cheese and refried beans.
12. Roll enchiladas and place them in a baking dish. Pour the sauce over the top and sprinkle remaining cheese over enchiladas.
13. Bake at 350 degrees for 30 minutes or until cheese is melted and enchilada sauce is hot.

Serves 4-5

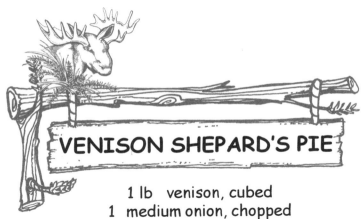

VENISON SHEPARD'S PIE

1 lb   venison, cubed
1 medium onion, chopped
1 small can of mushrooms
1 can cream of mushroom soup
1 can cream of celery soup
2 cans mixed vegetables, drained
minced garlic, to taste
1 bouillon cube, crushed
salt and pepper
mashed potatoes
shredded Colby or cheddar cheese

1. Brown the venison with the onion and mushrooms.
2. Mix venison with soups, mixed vegetables and seasonings and place in a casserole dish.
3. Add a layer of mashed potatoes to the top of the dish.
4. Bake covered at 350 degrees for 45 minutes.
5. Remove from oven, add a sprinkling of cheese to top of mashed potatoes, and return uncovered to oven for 10-15 minutes or until cheese is melted.

Serve with hot biscuits and salad. This is a good way to use up leftover mashed potatoes. For a variation you may add some chopped green pepper to the venison when you brown it.

Serves 4

VENISON STEAK

This recipe can be used with deer,
elk, or domestic beef.

seasoned salt
cornmeal
venison steaks
vegetable oil
dry onion soup mix
mushrooms (*fresh is best, but canned or dried can be used*)
beef broth

1. Add enough seasoned salt to the cornmeal so that it has an orange tint.
2. Coat dry steaks with cornmeal and place in refrigerator for $\frac{1}{2}$ hour.
3. Remove from refrigerator and cook in hot oil until crust starts to brown on both sides.
4. Place in baking dish.
   Sprinkle dry onion soup mix over steaks and add mushrooms.
5. Put enough broth in to keep steaks from drying out.
6. Bake covered at 300 degrees for $1\frac{1}{2}$ hours.
   Uncover and let bake for 15 more minutes.

Serve with baked potatoes and broccoli.

Serves 4

VENISON TERIYAKI SHISKABOB

Kabobs:

1-2 lbs stew venison
1-2 medium onions
1 red bell pepper
1 green bell pepper

Marinade:

1 C teriyaki sauce
$\frac{1}{4}$ C lemon juice
$\frac{1}{4}$ C lime juice
$\frac{1}{4}$ C orange juice (*optional*)
$\frac{1}{4}$ C pineapple juice (*optional*)
1 T jarred minced garlic
salt and pepper to taste

1. Dice meat into 2" cubes.
2. Chop onions and peppers into $1\frac{1}{2}$" squares.
3. Mix all marinade ingredients together. Pour marinade over meat and vegetables and let sit in the fridge for a couple of hours.
4. Skewer meat and veggies alternately, saving juice. (*If using wooden skewers remember to pre-soak them in water to avoid burning the skewers.*)
5. Cook on grill, brushing frequently with remaining juice, to whatever color/temperature desired. Medium-rare seems best for this cut and manner of cooking.

Serve over white rice.

Serves 4

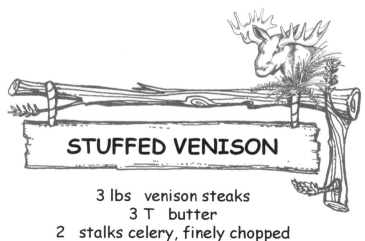

STUFFED VENISON

3 lbs   venison steaks
3 T   butter
2   stalks celery, finely chopped
1 C   onion, finely diced
1   green pepper, finely diced
2 C   bread crumbs
2 T   water
$\frac{1}{2}$ t   salt
$\frac{1}{4}$ t   pepper
$\frac{1}{4}$ t   poultry seasoning
2   6-oz cans tomato sauce
2 T   taco sauce

1. Pound steaks to $\frac{1}{4}$" thick.

2. Melt butter and sauté celery, onion and pepper until soft.

3. Mix in bowl with bread crumbs, salt, pepper and seasoning.
   Add water to make stick together.

4. Place stuffing mixture on steak and roll steak up.
   Fasten with toothpicks.

5. Browned stuffed steaks in oiled skillet.

6. Mix tomato sauce and taco sauce and pour over browned
   steaks.

7. Bake in covered dish at 350 degrees for 1 hour or until done.

DAGRIZ BEEF 'N' BEER BAR
3K CABBAGE ROLLS

24 cabbage leaves, trimmed
(*outside leaves from 2 large cabbages*)
1 28-oz can diced tomatoes, drained, juice reserved
3 C vegetable juice
1 14-oz can beef broth
3 T Worcestershire sauce
1 T salt
2½ lb ground beef, very lean
1 large onion, finely diced
1 large carrot, finely diced
1 medium green pepper, finely diced
3 celery ribs, finely diced
2 C precooked rice, divided
1 T garlic powder
1 T onion powder
1 t fresh black pepper
2 eggs
2 T dark brown sugar

DAGRIZ BEEF 'N' BEER BAR
3K CABBAGE ROLLS con't

1. Prepare the leaves by immersing the cabbage head in boiling water for 3 minutes. Cut the leaves free and remove from the stalk.

2. Cut away the thick vein in the center of each leaf.

3. In a large container combine the juice from the tomatoes, vegetable juice, beef broth, Worcestershire sauce and salt.

4. In a second container mix the meat, vegetables, 1 cup of the rice, and remaining seasonings.

5. Beat the eggs and add to the meat mixture. Combine well. Assure that the meat will hold together when forming a ball. If needed, a little vegetable juice may be added to this mixture to moisten.

6. Wrap a good-sized handful of the meat mixture in each leaf. Roll from the bottom and tuck in the ends.

7. Place the completed rolls in a large, shallow roasting pan or a Dutch oven if preparing out doors and pour the juice mixture over the rolls as evenly as possible. This should come just short of covering the rolls completely.

8. Mix the brown sugar and the drained tomatoes together until the sugar is well dissolved. Evenly distribute this over the top of the rolls. Cover the pan with foil.

9. Bake at 350 degrees for 1 hour or until cabbage is tender and the inside temperature of the roll is 165 degrees or higher. May also be cooked in slow crockpot for 6-8 hours.

Makes 20-24 rolls

WILD GAME MEATLOAF

2 lbs   ground venison, very lean
wild boar or javelina
1 lb   ground turkey meat, preferably wild turkey
½ lb   ground pork, preferably shoulder
2   large onions, diced
2   eggs, chicken or duck
¼ C   seasoned breadcrumbs
1 t   garlic powder or ½ clove garlic, finely diced
1 t   black pepper, coarse ground
¼ C   A-1 Sauce®
lard, bacon grease, or butter
4-6   slices of bacon

1. Mix all ingredients except bacon in a small crock, clay bowl, or bark container.
2. Let set in cold, spring fed creek or ice chest for 2 hours or so.
3. Liberally coat the inside of a cast-iron Dutch oven or covered cast-iron frying pan with lard, bacon grease or butter or with buffalo tallow rendered down to lard.
4. Form mixture into a loaf and place in greased Dutch oven or frying pan.
5. Have a fire burned down to hot coals about 3" deep.
6. Place bacon lengthways on top of loaf. Cover; place in the hot coals and cover with more coals.
7. Bake for 2-2½ hours, checking after 1½ hours. Use a whittled stick, free of bark, to pierce meatloaf and see if it is completely cooked through.

Serves 6

BARBECUED MOOSE PEPPER STEAK

6 small moose steaks
2 t meat tenderizer
½ C white wine
½ C red wine
2 t Worcestershire sauce
1 t marjoram
1 t thyme
3 T onion, finely diced
2 t pepper
salt to taste

1. Combine red and white wine, meat tenderizer, Worcestershire sauce, marjoram, thyme, and onion. Save ½ C to baste.
2. Pour over steaks and marinate 3-5 hours.
3. Add pepper and salt to taste.
4. Grill to desired doneness, basting with reserved sauce.

Serves 4-6

GRILLED BACON-WRAPPED BIG GAME

Deer, antelope, elk, moose or bear
can be used and is excellent when
prepared in this simple fashion.

1-1¼ lbs big-game round or rump pieces, ¾'''-1" thick
4-8 slices of bacon

1. Cut meat into 2" wide strips.
2. Wrap 1 or 2 slices bacon around each strip. Secure bacon with toothpicks.
3. When charcoal briquettes are covered with ash, spread them in grill. Place grate above hot coals. Grill meat strips to desired doneness, 4-7 minutes per side.

Serve as a main course, or as an appetizer for a wild-game dinner.

Serves 2-4

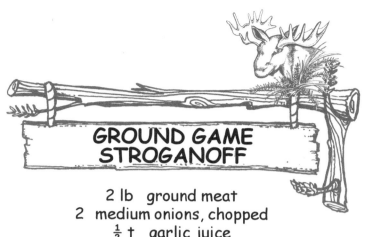

GROUND GAME STROGANOFF

2 lb   ground meat
2   medium onions, chopped
½ t   garlic juice
small can mushrooms
¼ t   pepper
1   can consommé
3 T   tomato paste
2½ t   salt
1½ C   sour cream
4 T   flour

1. Brown ground beef in skillet.
2. Add onions, garlic juice, mushrooms and pepper.
   Sauté until onion is golden brown.
3. Mix consommé, tomato paste, salt and sour cream.
   Add to beef.
4. Carefully add and mix in flour. Simmer until thickened.
5. Serve over cooked rice or noodles.

Serves 4-6

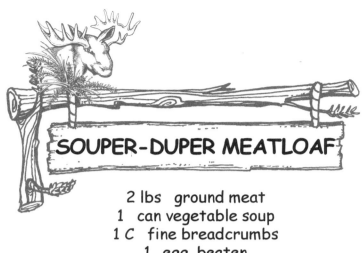

SOUPER-DUPER MEATLOAF

2 lbs   ground meat
1   can vegetable soup
1 C   fine breadcrumbs
1   egg, beaten
1 C   chopped onion
1 t   salt
dash of pepper

1. Combine all ingredients.

2. Shape into loaf.

3. Bake in greased pan at 350 degrees for $1\frac{1}{4}$ hours.

Serves 4-6

FRIED SQUIRREL

4 squirrels, quartered
3 C milk
4 T salt
1 C flour
pepper to taste
cooking oil
¼ stick butter
4 T orange juice

1. Soak quartered squirrels overnight in milk and salt.

2. Pat dry and roll in flour and pepper.

3. Fry in cooking oil.

4. Pour off drippings.

5. Add butter and orange juice to pan.

6. Cover and steam approximately 15 minutes.

Serves 2-4

MEXICAN RABBIT

1 rabbit, skinned and cleaned
1 can chili beans
½ t cayenne pepper
1 package Spanish rice mix
1 package taco seasoning mix
2 C cheddar cheese, shredded
2 C sour cream
tortilla chips

1. Simmer rabbit until it is falling off the bone.
   Let it cool and remove bones.

2. In skillet, mix rabbit, beans, cayenne pepper, taco mix and enough water to keep mixture from burning. Simmer for 20 minutes.

3. Stir together Spanish rice mix, 1 cup of water and rabbit-bean mixture. Pour into a large baking dish and top with one-third of the cheese.

4. Bake at 275 degrees for 45-60 minutes.

5. Remove from oven. Spread a layer of sour cream on top, followed by a layer of cheese, a layer of chips and another layer of cheese.

6. Return to oven until cheese is melted.
   Remove from oven and serve.

Serves 4-6

BARBECUED ANTELOPE

4 antelope steaks
1 t rosemary
1 t oregano
1 T pickling spice
$\frac{1}{3}$ C red wine
1 small garlic clove, chopped
1 t salt

1. Place meat in large saucepan and add all ingredients with water to cover.
2. Heat to boiling.
3. Reduce heat to simmer.
4. Cook 2 hours or until tender. Let sit about 15 minutes before serving.

Serves 2-4

WILD HOG

3-4 ham steaks, cut thick
teriyaki sauce
salt and pepper
garlic

1. Let steaks stand in seasoned teriyaki sauce at least 1 hour.
2. Place in crockpot and cover with teriyaki sauce.
3. Let simmer at least 5 hours or until falling apart.
4. Remove steaks and serve over steamed white rice.

Serve with fresh broccoli or any other fresh vegetables.

Serves 2

MARIAN'S DEER SAUSAGE AND RICE

1 lb   hot smoked sausage
1 lb   regular smoked sausage
1   large onion, finely chopped
1   large bell pepper, finely chopped
1   stalk celery, finely chopped (*at least 1 cup*)
1   can water chestnuts, finely chopped
2   packages dry chicken noodle soup
2 C   boiling water
2 C   raw rice
1   package slivered almonds

1. Sauté sausage in large pan or skillet. Drain, saving drippings.

2. Sauté chopped vegetables in sausage drippings.

3. Mix 2 cups boiling water with soup. Mix and boil about 7 minutes in large pan.

4. In large bowl, mix sausage, vegetables, soup, and raw rice (*if mixture seems dry, add ¼ cup water*) and put in a covered baking dish.

5. Bake 300 degrees for 1½ hours. Arrange on large platter and top with slivered almonds.

Serves 2-4

BAGGED BEAR

Bear is one of the finest game meats. It is often maligned because of ill preparation. Bear is rich, sweet and tender with no muscle marble. Braising and high humidity roasting in a bag works best for general cuts. Bear should NEVER be cooked with the bone or its own fat or sinew. Only fish-eating bears have a naturally strong flavor. Bears that eat a great deal of bitter acorns may be tangy too. Berry-eating bears are quite tasty. As with all game, bear should be cooled ASAP. For best results take the time to bone and trim prior to freezing your meat. For least game flavor, use the buttermilk soak.

2-4 lbs   bear roast
buttermilk or regular milk, if desired
1   large onion, coarsely chopped
1   slivered garlic clove (*optional*)
1   package dried onion soup
1 T   flour mushroom gravy
Fresh or canned mushrooms
1   Reynolds® oven bag large size
(*find these in the foil aisle*)
Cornstarch or flour

BAGGED BEAR con't

1. Bone out all fat sinew and silver skin.
2. Soak refrigerated overnight in buttermilk or regular milk if desired.
3. Shake off milk. Marinate if you like, not required.
4. Spike roast with slivered garlic if desired.
5. Preheat oven to 350 degrees.
6. Put soup mix and flour or gravy packet, and the chopped onion in bag and shake.
7. Place bag in a roasting pan with 2" sides, just big enough to accommodate the size of the roast. Add fresh or canned mushrooms. If using canned, reserve liquid and add enough more water to make $\frac{3}{4}$ C. If using fresh add $\frac{3}{4}$ C water.
8. Slosh pan gently to wet dry ingredients on the bottom of pan. Put roast in on top of onions and mushies and flip a few times to get seasoning on the roast. Close bag and poke 4 or 5 small holes in top of sealed bag.
9. If possible, put a meat thermometer into the center of roast. Roast to 165 degrees or about 2 hours for a 4-lb roast. Remove roast from bag and let cool 10 minutes.
10. Reserve all gravy from bag and thicken in a pan over medium heat with cornstarch or flour if desired.

Serve with the gravy and mashed potatoes, green beans and fresh rolls.

You can also use a Dutch oven with coals. Use a bit more liquid and cook slow to medium heat a bit longer. If using the Dutch oven, test the meat after $1\frac{1}{2}$-2 hours.

You can use any type of game roast with this recipe: tied goose breast, elk or deer neck roast (*bone and tie for best results*).

DA LIMP NOODLE

A hearty Stroganoff-style dish that is absolutely delicious and stretches to feed a crowd. As a matter of fact that is how it was invented and named: at a potluck in Keysville, Virginia, in June 2002 at a gathering of North American Hunting Club members.

2 lbs Johnsonville Stadium-Style Bratwurst
2 large packages extra-wide egg noodles
(24 oz - 32 oz total weight)
1 large, flat Vidalia onion, sliced very thin
1 lb portobello mushrooms, sliced thin
(*dish is prettier if the gills are removed*)
1-2 T flour
$\frac{1}{2}$ T garlic powder
1 qt sour cream
1 qt white wine
2 T high heat oil (*peanut or olive*)
coarse sea salt and fresh ground pepper to taste

DA LIMP NOODLE con't

1. Set sufficient water to boil in accordance with the package directions of the noodles. A large pinch of coarse sea salt may be added to speed boiling and help flavor the noodles.

2. Heat a large skillet (12-14") and add the oil. Immediately place the brats in the oil and begin to move them around to completely brown them. This should take about 10 minutes. Remove the brats from the pan and allow them to rest at least 5 minutes.

3. Check the water and when appropriate add the noodles. After the brats have rested, slice them into $\frac{1}{2}$" pieces. Set them aside for later use.

4. Add the sliced onions to the skillet and reduce the heat slightly to a medium high. Allow the onions to just begin to turn clear, then add the mushrooms. Raise the heat slightly closer to high. The vegetables should begin to absorb the drippings from the pan.

5. When this happens return the sliced brats to the pan and allow them to cook for about 5 minutes while continually stirring. If the pan appears to be dry additional cooking oil may be added a half-tablespoon at a time. Add no more than one additional full tablespoon.

6. Sprinkle half the flour over the contents of the pan and add the garlic powder. Stir to combine well and to absorb the flour. Add the sour cream and combine well.

7. Add the wine a little at a time to achieve a consistency about like a sausage gravy or a bit thinner. This should take about half of the wine or a bit more.

8. When the noodles are finished drain them well, add them to the sauce and combine well. Test and adjust seasonings as desired. Check the sauce. If it is too thick add a little more wine and combine. If too thin (*doesn't coat the noodles*) sprinkle a little of the remaining flour over the dish and combine well. Do not use more flour than what was left over from the original recipe measure because too much raw flour will ruin the dish.

Serves 10-15

PANCIT CANTON-COMPLEX NOODLE DISH À LA PAWS

Although this is not my creation I have modified the traditional dish quite a bit and therefore claim it as my own. It may be prepared out doors very easily, but the aroma attracts campers from all over, so use caution!!

Note: This is a complex recipe with many ingredients. Please read through carefully before you begin.

1 fresh 3-to-4 pound chicken, cut into 6 pieces, skin and fat removed. Precook the chicken. Boil in a large pot with 1 medium-sized onion, 2 stalks celery and 8 peppercorns. Add enough water to cover the contents of the pot. Cook until chicken is tender but not falling off the bone. Remove the meat, de-bone. When thoroughly cooled, dice into $\frac{1}{2}$" cubes. Reserve the stock! (*There should be approximately 8 cups.*)

2 T sesame oil mixed with 2 T extra-virgin olive oil
(*or use 4 T peanut oil*)
1 medium-sized sweet onion, thinly sliced
(*such as Vidalia or Maui Sweet*)
2 cloves garlic, crushed
1 lb pork, sliced into thin strips
($\frac{1}{4}$"*thick x* $\frac{1}{2}$" *long and* $\frac{1}{2}$" *wide,*
or just slightly smaller than the chicken cubes above)
1 C shrimp, precooked, deveined and shelled
(*20 medium boiled whole for 3 minutes*)
$\frac{1}{2}$ lb mussels or scallops (*optional*)
1 14-oz can straw mushrooms
1 8-10 oz can of sliced water chestnuts
2 C julienned bok choy or fresh green cabbage
1 large carrot, julienned
12 oz fresh snow peas or sugar snap peas in the pods
4 T soy sauce
1 T patis (*fermented fish sauce, optional*)
2 T sea salt
1 t freshly ground black pepper
2 8-oz pkgs Pancit Canton or lo mein noodles

PANCIT CANTON-COMPLEX NOODLE DISH À LA PAWS con't

Garnish:
½ C finely chopped green onion
4 limes

1. After all ingredients have been gathered and prepared including the preparation of the chicken, pork, and shrimp, heat a large pan or wok. Add about half of the oil mixture and sauté the onion and garlic until the onion is transparent.
2. Add the pork and cook over high heat until browned and tender. Add the chicken and the remaining oil and cook until just beginning to brown.
3. Add half of the chicken stock. Boil for about three minutes. Add all of the seasonings. Simmer for about another three minutes.
4. Add shrimp, mussels and scallops (*if using*), mushrooms, water chestnuts, bok choy, carrot and snow peas and simmer, covered, for 3 minutes.
5. Add the remaining stock. Adjust the seasonings to taste and add the noodles. Mix thoroughly, remove from heat and cover. Let stand until noodles are soft completely through. Noodles will absorb about 60 percent of the broth. Toss noodles before serving.
6. Serve in bowls garnished with the chopped green onion, a slice of lime, and a squeeze of fresh lime juice.

Serve with plain rice and egg rolls or lumpia on the side.

Serves 6-8

ROGUE RIVER SPECIAL

1 C white rice
2 C water
carrots, peeled and sliced
into quarter-size rounds
2 stalks broccoli, separated into flowerets
and stems coarsely chopped
1 C cauliflower flowerets
1 lb venison sausage
(*ham or regular sausage may be substituted*)
1 onion, chopped
½ lb mushrooms, sliced
1 zucchini, chopped
12 eggs, beaten
salt, pepper, parsley, hot sauce, granulated garlic
2 C grated cheddar cheese, Swiss or combination

1. Put rice and water in a lidded pot. Bring to a boil, then reduce heat and simmer until rice is cooked and water is absorbed, about 20 minutes.

2. While rice is cooking, steam the carrots, broccoli and cauliflower for 5 minutes or until tender. Remove from heat and set aside.

3. Brown the sausage with the mushrooms and the onion. Just before done throw in the zucchini, carrots, broccoli and cauliflower. Sauté just a bit longer.

4. Add the cooked rice and stir together.

Add the eggs and seasonings and cook until set. Add the cheese. Turn off heat and let the cheese melt. Serve immediately.

Serves 6-8

Groveland Cottage

124

TATER CHOP SUEY

potatoes
dry macaroni
mushrooms
onion
spaghetti sauce
shredded cheese
sour cream, optional

1. Cut up a couple of potatoes into 1" cubes.
2. Boil enough dry macaroni to accommodate however many people you are serving.
3. Fry up the chunks of potatoes until soft and browned.
4. Add your favorite mushrooms, and a few chunks of onion to brown with potatoes.
5. Mix together macaroni and potato mixture in a baking pan.
6. Stir in favorite spaghetti sauce and top with shredded cheese.
7. Bake at 375 degrees for 10 minutes.

This is great served with a little sour cream.

Serves 4

HUNTERS' TAMALES

Filling:

1½ lbs beef or pork, stewed and shredded
(*or chicken, turkey or venison*)
1 T lard or shortening
1 T flour
½ C red chili powder*
2 C meat broth
½ t salt
⅛ t dried oregano
¼ t ground cumin
½ t garlic salt

1. Combine meat and shortening in a large skillet and fry at medium heat until browned.
2. Add the flour to meat and cook for 1 minute, stirring constantly.
3. Add chili powder, broth and seasonings to meat. Cook at medium heat for approximately 30 minutes, stirring constantly until mixture has thickened.

*Varied amounts may be used according to your taste. Substitute ½ C chopped green chilies to make green chili tamales.

Yields 6 cups

HUNTERS' TAMALES con't

Masa (Cornmeal Mixture):

6 C masa harina
3½ C warm water
2 C shortening
2 t salt

1. Combine the masa harina and water in a large mixing bowl. Set aside.
2. Cream shortening and salt in a medium bowl using mixer at medium speed.
3. Add the creamed shortening mixture to the masa and mix well.

Tamales:

60-80 dried cornhusks
water
masa, prepared as directed above
filling, prepared as directed above

1. Rinse cornhusks and soak in warm water until pliable.
2. Spread the center portion of each husk with about 2 T of masa mixture. Top with 1 T or more of meat filling.
3. Fold the sides of the husk toward the center, the bottom of the husk up, and the top down. Tie each tamale with a strip of cornhusk.
4. Pour 2" of water into a large steamer. Arrange tamales on a rack in steamer above the water level.
5. Steam tamales for 45 minutes. May also be steamed in a pressure cooker for 20 minutes at 15 pounds pressure.

Makes 5-6 dozen

May be kept frozen in freezer up to 6 months.

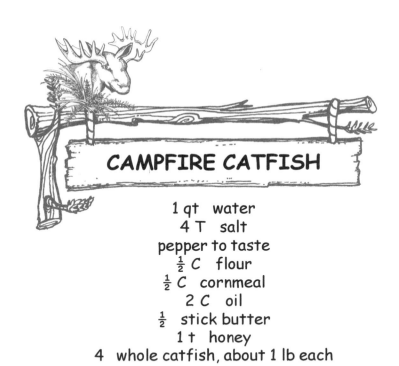

CAMPFIRE CATFISH

1 qt   water
4 T   salt
pepper to taste
½ C   flour
½ C   cornmeal
2 C   oil
½   stick butter
1 t   honey
4   whole catfish, about 1 lb each

1. Soak catfish in water and salt for at least 2 hours.

2. Remove from water, pat dry, and add salt and pepper to taste.

3. Combine flour and cornmeal. Coat fish with this mixture.

4. Heat oil, butter and honey to high temperature for frying.

5. Fry fish fast, about 10 minutes each side.

Serves 2-4

ONE POTS

GOOSE STEW

1 goose,
skinned and cut into cubes
margarine or butter
Worcestershire sauce
1 pkg   dried onion soup mix
2 C   beef broth, divided
2 C   chicken broth, divided
seasoned salt
liquid smoke
4   large peeled potatoes, cut into cubes
3 C   small whole carrots
2 C   celery, cut into bite-sized pieces
2 C   frozen or fresh peas

1. Brown goose cubes in melted butter mixed with Worcestershire sauce.
2. Mix onion soup $\frac{1}{2}$ strength with water and put in large crockpot.
3. Add 1 C each beef and chicken broth. Put in browned cubes and add seasoned salt to taste.
4. Add 3 capfuls liquid smoke and cook on high for about 3 hours.
5. Add vegetables (*except peas*) and remaining broth. Taste to check flavor. It should be a little strong because the vegetables will add water.
6. Cook another 3 hours on low heat.
7. Strain broth off to thicken or thicken in pot.
8. Add peas and cook on low for an additional hour.

Serve over buttered noodles.

Serves 2-4

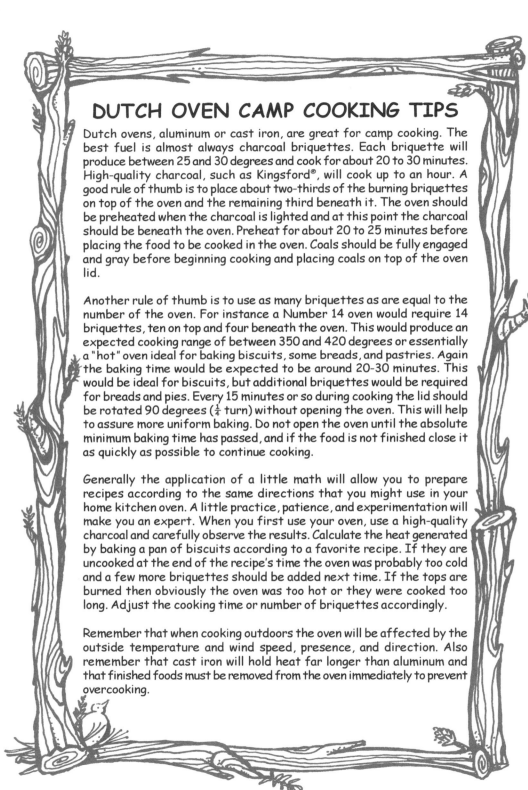

DUTCH OVEN CAMP COOKING TIPS

Dutch ovens, aluminum or cast iron, are great for camp cooking. The best fuel is almost always charcoal briquettes. Each briquette will produce between 25 and 30 degrees and cook for about 20 to 30 minutes. High-quality charcoal, such as Kingsford®, will cook up to an hour. A good rule of thumb is to place about two-thirds of the burning briquettes on top of the oven and the remaining third beneath it. The oven should be preheated when the charcoal is lighted and at this point the charcoal should be beneath the oven. Preheat for about 20 to 25 minutes before placing the food to be cooked in the oven. Coals should be fully engaged and gray before beginning cooking and placing coals on top of the oven lid.

Another rule of thumb is to use as many briquettes as are equal to the number of the oven. For instance a Number 14 oven would require 14 briquettes, ten on top and four beneath the oven. This would produce an expected cooking range of between 350 and 420 degrees or essentially a "hot" oven ideal for baking biscuits, some breads, and pastries. Again the baking time would be expected to be around 20-30 minutes. This would be ideal for biscuits, but additional briquettes would be required for breads and pies. Every 15 minutes or so during cooking the lid should be rotated 90 degrees ($\frac{1}{4}$ turn) without opening the oven. This will help to assure more uniform baking. Do not open the oven until the absolute minimum baking time has passed, and if the food is not finished close it as quickly as possible to continue cooking.

Generally the application of a little math will allow you to prepare recipes according to the same directions that you might use in your home kitchen oven. A little practice, patience, and experimentation will make you an expert. When you first use your oven, use a high-quality charcoal and carefully observe the results. Calculate the heat generated by baking a pan of biscuits according to a favorite recipe. If they are uncooked at the end of the recipe's time the oven was probably too cold and a few more briquettes should be added next time. If the tops are burned then obviously the oven was too hot or they were cooked too long. Adjust the cooking time or number of briquettes accordingly.

Remember that when cooking outdoors the oven will be affected by the outside temperature and wind speed, presence, and direction. Also remember that cast iron will hold heat far longer than aluminum and that finished foods must be removed from the oven immediately to prevent overcooking.

DUTCH OVEN ROAST VENISON

3 lbs   venison roast
2-3 T   bacon drippings
3   strips of bacon
1   onion, sliced and separated into rings
$\frac{1}{2}$ C   hot water
$10\frac{3}{4}$-oz can   tomato soup
$\frac{1}{3}$ t   garlic
$\frac{1}{2}$ t   salt
$\frac{1}{4}$ t   pepper
$\frac{1}{4}$ t   dried basil
$\frac{1}{3}$ C   cider vinegar
3 T   flour

1. In Dutch oven, sear meat in bacon drippings.

2. Lay strips of bacon across roast, securing with toothpicks.

3. Hang onion slices over toothpicks.

4. Add hot water, tomato soup, garlic, salt, pepper and basil to Dutch oven. Cover and simmer for 2-3 hours or until tender.

5. Thicken pan juices and add vinegar and flour to make gravy if desired.

Serves 6-8

BAIZE'S SOUTHWESTERN WHITE CHILI

$\frac{2}{3}$ C   dried northern white beans
2 14-oz cans   chicken broth
2 t   vegetable oil
1 C   chopped onion
2   garlic cloves, minced
1 lb   ground turkey
1 C   corn, drained
1 T   chili powder
$\frac{1}{2}$ t   salt
$\frac{1}{4}$ t   ground cumin
1 4$\frac{1}{2}$-oz can   chopped green chilies
2 T   cornmeal

1. Sort and wash beans, place in large pan. Cover with water, bring to boil and cook 2 minutes. Remove from heat, cover and let stand 1 hour. Drain beans and return to pan.

2. Add broth and bring to boil. Reduce heat and simmer approximately 1 hour, until beans are tender. Remove $\frac{1}{4}$ cup of beans, drain and mash with fork, then return mashed beans to pan.

3. Coat a nonstick skillet with cooking spray. Add oil and heat until oil is hot. Add onion and garlic and sauté until tender. Add ground turkey and cook until no longer pink.

4. Add turkey mixture, corn, chili powder, salt, cumin and green chilies to beans and bring to boil. Reduce heat and simmer uncovered for 20-30 minutes.

5. Sprinkle cornmeal over chili and cook until thick, stirring frequently.

Can be made with ground chicken or 4 chicken breasts, cubed

Serves 4

BUFFALO ROUNDUP CHILI

2 lb ground buffalo
1 T oil
salt and pepper to taste
2 cans red kidney beans
1 can chili-ets (*seasoned beans*)
1 can stewed tomatoes
1 small can tomato sauce
1 medium onion
1 bay leaf
2 t chili powder
2 t cumin
1 t Worcestershire sauce
1 jar mild all-natural salsa
2 T brown sugar

1. In large pot, brown ground buffalo in oil until done.

2. Add remaining ingredients and cook for 1 hour.

Tip: During the last ten minutes of simmering, add two
heaping T of Nestle Quick®.

Serves 4-6

CAMP "FIRE" TOUCAN (*TWO CAN*) STEW

2 15-17-oz cans cut carrots
2 15-17-oz cans cut asparagus
2 T jalapeno peppers, diced
2 t finely diced garlic
salt and pepper to taste
2 15-17-oz cans mixed vegetables
2 26-30-oz cans stewed tomatoes
2 cans "HOT" Spam® cut into $\frac{1}{2}$" cubes
2 15-17-oz cans whole potatoes, cut into $\frac{1}{2}$" cubes

1. In a 4-qt or larger pot combine one can of each ingredient in the order shown.
2. When the consistency of the stew seems proper, begin to drain the water from each additional can of vegetables before adding the vegetables to the pot.
3. Add seasonings, combine well and bring the stew to a quick simmer.
4. Reduce the heat to a medium or slow simmer and allow to heat through for about 5 minutes. Test for seasoning and adjust as required.
5. Serve with crackers and cheese.

This recipe will serve 6 to 10 hungry campers.

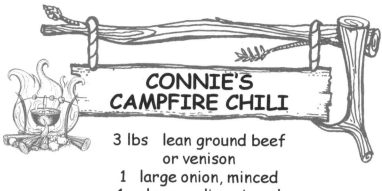

CONNIE'S CAMPFIRE CHILI

3 lbs   lean ground beef
or venison
1   large onion, minced
1   clove garlic, minced
1   can stewed tomatoes
1   large can V-8 Juice®
2   packages chili mix
1 T   chili powder
2 cans   pinto beans
salt and pepper
grated cheese and onions

1. Brown meat, onion and garlic until meat is no longer pink.

2. Add tomatoes, V-8 Juice®, chili mix and chili powder.

3. Simmer for 30–40 minutes.

4. Add pinto beans along with salt and pepper to taste.

Simmer 15–20 minutes. Serve with grated cheese and onions sprinkled on top.

Serves 8–10

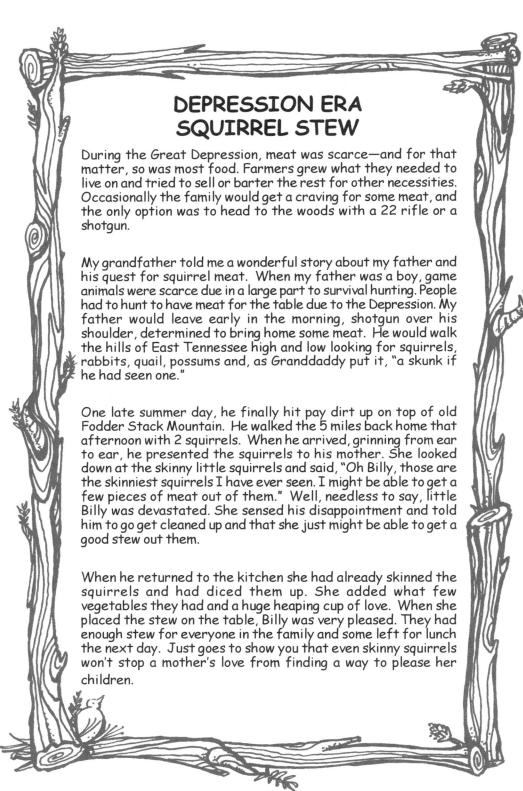

DEPRESSION ERA SQUIRREL STEW

During the Great Depression, meat was scarce—and for that matter, so was most food. Farmers grew what they needed to live on and tried to sell or barter the rest for other necessities. Occasionally the family would get a craving for some meat, and the only option was to head to the woods with a 22 rifle or a shotgun.

My grandfather told me a wonderful story about my father and his quest for squirrel meat. When my father was a boy, game animals were scarce due in a large part to survival hunting. People had to hunt to have meat for the table due to the Depression. My father would leave early in the morning, shotgun over his shoulder, determined to bring home some meat. He would walk the hills of East Tennessee high and low looking for squirrels, rabbits, quail, possums and, as Granddaddy put it, "a skunk if he had seen one."

One late summer day, he finally hit pay dirt up on top of old Fodder Stack Mountain. He walked the 5 miles back home that afternoon with 2 squirrels. When he arrived, grinning from ear to ear, he presented the squirrels to his mother. She looked down at the skinny little squirrels and said, "Oh Billy, those are the skinniest squirrels I have ever seen. I might be able to get a few pieces of meat out of them." Well, needless to say, little Billy was devastated. She sensed his disappointment and told him to go get cleaned up and that she just might be able to get a good stew out them.

When he returned to the kitchen she had already skinned the squirrels and had diced them up. She added what few vegetables they had and a huge heaping cup of love. When she placed the stew on the table, Billy was very pleased. They had enough stew for everyone in the family and some left for lunch the next day. Just goes to show you that even skinny squirrels won't stop a mother's love from finding a way to please her children.

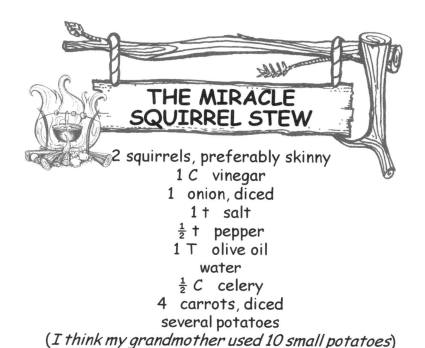

THE MIRACLE SQUIRREL STEW

2 squirrels, preferably skinny
1 C   vinegar
1   onion, diced
1 t   salt
½ t   pepper
1 T   olive oil
water
½ C   celery
4   carrots, diced
several potatoes
(*I think my grandmother used 10 small potatoes*)

1. Wash and skin the squirrels. Wash again and cut meat into small pieces. Mix vinegar, onion, salt and pepper in a pot. Add the squirrel meat and cover with water. Allow to sit for 2 hours.

2. Remove squirrel and brown in oil in skillet. Combine browned squirrel meat, celery, carrots and potatoes in pot and cover with water.

4. Cover and cook until tender.

DEERCAMP DAN'S GOULASH

1 large yellow onion, chopped
1 medium bell pepper, chopped
1 can tomato sauce
1 small can whole kernel corn, drained
1 can ranch-style beans
1 can Rotel® tomatoes
salt and pepper
$\frac{1}{3}$ C noodles, cooked and drained
$\frac{1}{4}$-$\frac{1}{2}$ lbs Velveeta® cheese, grated
2 lbs ground beef or deer meat

1. Brown meat, onions and bell pepper in pan until meat is done. Drain.
2. Add tomato sauce, corn, beans, tomatoes, and salt and pepper to taste.
3. Stir and simmer on low heat for 20-25 minutes.
4. Add cooked noodles and cheese; stir and heat until cheese is melted.

Serve with cornbread or over Fritos®.

Serves 4-6

MARIAN'S DEER ROAST

1   deer roast
garlic cloves
Microwave Kitchen Bouquet® spray
bottled teriyaki sauce
1   onion, sliced
1   green bell pepper, sliced
1-2 cans   Campbells® Golden Mushroom Soup
(*depends on size of meat*)
dried parsley flakes
ground black pepper
garlic powder
seasoned salt
Worcestershire sauce

1. Cut small slits in deer roast and insert garlic cloves to taste.
   Spray Kitchen Bouquet® on meat.
   Marinate in teriyaki sauce overnight.

2. Drain off marinade. Put roast in crockpot and add the
   remaining ingredients.

3. Cook on low for 10-12 hours. Soup will make gravy.

For barbecue-flavored deer roast follow above directions but
use water instead of soup. Cut cooked meat into bite-size pieces
and return to crockpot. Add Kraft Barbecue Sauce with Honey®
and stir.

Serves 4-6

FRYING PAN SUPPER

1 lb   hamburger
or other ground meat
1   small onion, chopped
2 C   potatoes, cut into strips
2 C   shredded cabbage
2 C   diced celery
salt
½ C   water

1. In large frying pan brown hamburger and onion.

2. Add potatoes, cabbage and celery. Sprinkle with salt.

3. Add water. Cover and simmer for 20 minutes or until vegetables are done.

Serves 2-4

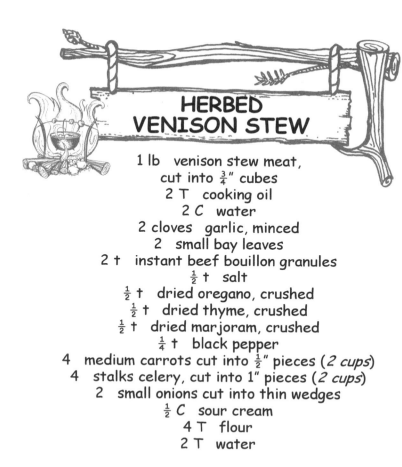

HERBED VENISON STEW

1 lb   venison stew meat,
cut into $\frac{3}{4}$" cubes
2 T   cooking oil
2 C   water
2 cloves   garlic, minced
2   small bay leaves
2 t   instant beef bouillon granules
$\frac{1}{2}$ t   salt
$\frac{1}{2}$ t   dried oregano, crushed
$\frac{1}{2}$ t   dried thyme, crushed
$\frac{1}{2}$ t   dried marjoram, crushed
$\frac{1}{4}$ t   black pepper
4   medium carrots cut into $\frac{1}{2}$" pieces (*2 cups*)
4   stalks celery, cut into 1" pieces (*2 cups*)
2   small onions cut into thin wedges
$\frac{1}{2}$ C   sour cream
4 T   flour
2 T   water

1. In a 2-qt saucepan brown meat in hot oil. Remove from heat.

2. Add 2 C water, garlic, bay leaves, bouillon granules, salt, oregano, thyme, marjoram and pepper. Bring mixture to a boil. Reduce heat and simmer, covered, for 30 minutes.

3. Add carrots, celery and onions. Cover and simmer about 25 minutes more, until meat and vegetables are tender. Remove bay leaves.

4. Combine sour cream, flour and the 2 T water. Blend about 1 C of the hot mixture into sour cream mixture. Return it to remaining hot mixture. Cook and stir until thickened and bubbly.

Any red meat can be used. Good served with hot biscuits or cornbread!

Serves 4

HUNTERS' FAVORITE CHILI

Set out bowls of shredded Cheddar cheese and sour cream, and plenty of crackers, to top this hearty chili.

3 lbs   ground big game meat
3   medium onions, chopped
3   medium green peppers, chopped
½ C   chopped celery
2 T   bacon fat or vegetable oil
1   28-oz can whole tomatoes, undrained
2 T   dried parsley flakes
2 T   chili powder
1 t   salt
1 t   pepper
½ t   garlic powder
2   15½-oz cans kidney beans, undrained
1   16-oz can pinto beans, undrained

1. In Dutch oven, brown meat over medium heat, stirring occasionally. Remove from heat and set aside.

2. In large skillet, cook and stir onions, green peppers and celery in bacon fat over medium heat until tender.

3. Add vegetable mixture and all remaining ingredients except beans to meat in Dutch oven. Heat to boiling, then reduce heat and cover. Simmer 1 hour to blend flavors.

4. Stir in beans. Cook, uncovered, 30 minutes longer.

Serves 8-10

NEW ENGLAND CLAM CHOWDER

½ lb   bacon or salt pork
2   medium onions, chopped or diced
5   potatoes, peeled and cubed to ½"
1   52-oz can of clams, or fresh shucked coarsely chopped clams,
about 3 brimming pints; reserve all juice whichever you use
¼ C   flour
3 C   milk*
1 T   parsley flakes, fresh or dry
4 or 5   hard-boiled eggs, peeled and chopped (*optional*)
salt and pepper to taste
5 T   butter

1. In a heavy skillet over medium heat fry bacon until fairly crisp. While this cooks you can get the onions and potatoes ready.
2. When bacon is done, remove and set aside. Sauté onions in bacon drippings over medium heat until clear.
3. Spoon off any excess bacon grease. Add potatoes and clam juice. Simmer until the potatoes are just tender.
4. Transfer to large soup pot.
5. Whisk flour into milk and add to the pot. Heat, stirring often, until it just bubbles and starts to get nice and thick. You can add more flour mixed with some milk if it's not getting thick enough.
6. Crumble and add the bacon, parsley and salt and pepper to taste, stirring all the while.
7. Add the eggs (*if using*) and clams when the right thickness is reached. Keep stirring over low/medium until the clams are hot and it wants to bubble again.
Add the butter and stir until melted. Serve.

* You can use reconstituted powdered milk if you are away from a refrigerator or half-and-half if you are indulgent.

Serves 4

PAWCLAWS' SPECIAL CHICKEN RICE SOUP

This dish may be prepared in camp; however, be scrupulously aware of cleanliness and that a lot of space and cooking surfaces are required.

Set a 12-qt or larger stock pot with a lid, a 10" or 12" skillet with a lid, an 8-10 qt pot with a lid and a tall 4-qt pot with a lid on the stove. Gather your cutting board, chef's knife, vegetable peeler, paring knife, and boning knife, and pile up your carrots, onions, cabbage, celery, rice, chicken, etc. Get a cup of fresh hot coffee and take a deep breath, 'cause you are going to be busy for a while!

PHASE 1 - Preparing the Vegetables and Vegetable Stock
6 qts fresh cold water
4 C celery (*about 12 stalks*)
4 C carrots (*about 8 medium*)
½ hard medium cabbage
1½ large Vidalia onions

PHASE 2 - Preparing the Rice
4 C freshly prepared vegetable stock
2 C long-grain basmati rice

PHASE 3 - Preparing the Chicken Stock
1 4-5 lb roasting chicken
sufficient vegetable stock to cover (*about 4 qts*)

PHASE 4- Finishing the Soup

4 qts   chicken stock, reserved from above
4-6 C   vegetable stock, reserved from above
4 C   cooked rice
2-3 C   diced chicken meat
$2\frac{1}{2}$ C   diced Vidalia onion
$2\frac{1}{2}$ C   diced cabbage
2 C   diced carrot
2 C   diced celery
2 T   salt
1 T   Salt-Free 17®
1 t   MSG or Accent®
1 t   black pepper, freshly cracked
1 t   garlic powder
1 t   fresh basil, chopped
1 t   fresh marjoram, chopped
1 t   ground coriander

Procedure:

I like to prepare this soup on a Monday because I can pare my raw vegetable snacks for the week at the same time and prepare a really nice treat for the dogs as well. The soup will last for three or four days, and nobody complains about the leftovers!

1. Wash, peel and pare all of the vegetables in Phase 1.
    Place the peelings and trimmings into the large stockpot and fill with cold water. Bring the pot to a boil while covered. At a full boil, reduce the pot to a simmer and allow to continue cooking for the next 2 hours while covered. This may be cooked longer if desired.

2. Once the stock has cooked sufficiently to extract the flavors and color from the vegetable scraps, place 4 C of the liquid into the rice pot. Bring the liquid to a boil, add the rice, stir in and reduce the heat to low. Cover and weight the lid and allow the rice to cook at low heat for 20 minutes. Then turn off the heat and allow the rice to remain covered until the final preparation phase. It must remain covered for no less than 1 full hour.

3. Allow the remaining stock to continue cooking over low heat while the rice is cooking and you prepare the chicken and vegetables for the soup. You may add more water to the stock as well if so desired.

4. Meanwhile, wash the chicken and remove the giblets and place them in the sauté pan or skillet. Cut the chicken into 6 pieces and remove the skin from all of the pieces except the wings. Place the skin and wings in the skillet to render. Trim the fat from the chicken meat and place this in the skillet as well. Place the chicken meat, two breasts, two legs, two thighs, and back into the remaining empty pot and add sufficient vegetable stock to cover the meat. Bring the pot to a boil, cover with the lid, reduce the heat to low, and allow to cook for 20 minutes. The meat should be tender but not falling from the bone. Then remove the meat from the pot to a platter and allow to cool for about a half hour. While the chicken is cooking, attend both the skillet and chicken pot as you prepare the vegetables.

5. Mince the vegetables into very small pieces about the size of the rice grains or slightly larger. Prepare all of the onion, all of the cabbage, half of the carrot, and half of the celery in this manner. (*Cut the remaining celery and carrot into sticks to serve as raw snacks later. They may be kept fresh up to a week in a plastic dish with a sealed lid. The stalk of the cabbage may also be saved and sliced for snacking.*)

6. When the chicken is cooled, remove the meat from the bone and cut into large diced pieces, about $\frac{1}{4}$" each. The meat should be retained in the refrigerator and the bones returned to the chicken stock to improve the quality of the stock. Continue cooking the stock for an hour or so.

7. When the fat, giblets and wings have browned and cooked through in the skillet, they may be set aside for either a cook's treat or added to the pet's evening meal. Remove the meat from the bones if served to the pet. The bones from the wings may be added to the stockpot. Remove the bones from the chicken stock and discard after an hour minimum.

8. Place the diced vegetables into the pot, return the pot to a boil and allow to cook for 10 minutes at a quick simmer while covered.

9. Add the rice a cup at a time, assuring that the soup does not become too thick. Additional vegetable stock may be added as desired. Break the rice up into individual grains as much as possible.

10. Allow the soup to heat through for about 5 minutes, then add the chicken meat. Again, heat through for about 5 minutes. Add the seasonings and incorporate. Adjust the density of the soup by adding more rice to thicken or vegetable stock to thin. When the desired density is achieved, adjust seasonings to taste.

11. Remove from heat and allow to remain covered an hour before serving.

12. Keep leftovers in the refrigerator. The soup will improve during the next two days.

13. Serve with fresh French or garlic bread and a crisp green salad.
    Any remaining vegetable stock may be saved for later use by freezing.

Note: Chicken may be replaced with very lean beef or venison.

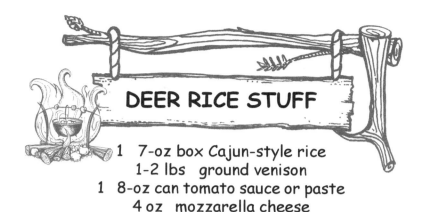

DEER RICE STUFF

1 7-oz box Cajun-style rice
1-2 lbs ground venison
1 8-oz can tomato sauce or paste
4 oz mozzarella cheese

1. Prepare Cajun rice as directed.

2. Brown the ground venison in a pan.

3. Layer rice and browned ground venison in a 10" square glass pan. Place rice in bottom, then add ground venison and top with tomato sauce.

4. Place dish in oven at 350 degrees for 10 to 15 minutes.

5. Remove dish and add mozzarella cheese to top. Place dish back in oven until cheese has melted.

Serves 3-4

PHEASANT CORN CHOWDER

This Amish-style soup is made extra special by the use of the egg dumplings or "rivles." In a pinch you can use packaged egg noodles, but it won't be the same. Give the rivles a try! You won't be sorry.

For the stock and soup:

1   clean pheasant, wild turkey, or chicken
1-2   garlic cloves, finely minced
2   onions, chopped
4   carrots, peeled and sliced
4   celery stalks, chopped
2-3 cans   kernel corn, undrained
1 pt   milk
some leftover flour from the rivles
4   hardboiled eggs, peeled and diced (*optional*)
salt and pepper
parsley
poultry seasoning or some sage, thyme and rosemary (*optional*)
soup base or bouillon cubes (*optional*)

1. Rinse the fowl and immerse in a stockpot with garlic in lightly salted and peppered water just covering the bird.

2. Cover and simmer for 10 minutes. Lengthen this initial time for bigger birds.

3. Remove lid and spoon off any foam or scum and add the onion, carrots, celery, and canned corn with juice, a bit more pepper and $\frac{1}{2}$ teaspoon of poultry seasoning if desired. Add more water sparingly to keep everything covered.

4. Cover and simmer for about 20 to 30 minutes, stirring occasionally. While the fowl is simmering, make the rivles (*recipe follows*).

5. Remove the fowl when cooked through—leg will pull off with firm pressure but not show pink juice. Set aside to cool. You should have about a gallon or so of stock. Add some water just so you have enough to boil the rivles later. Taste the stock and add additional seasoning if needed. Add the parsley. A few bouillon cubes or some soup base can be added, if you like, especially if you had to add water. Keep stock simmering with lid on until the rivles are ready to cook.

6. Prepare rivles.

PHEASANT CORN
CHOWDER con't

Rivles:

1 C flour
1 scant T salt
pinch baking powder (*optional*)
1 egg
oil (*optional*)

1. Mix flour, salt and pinch of baking powder in a medium bowl.

2. Make a hole in the middle for the flour and add the egg and a teaspoon of oil to the depression. Mix with fork from the middle to the sides until all flour is incorporated. The dough should be stiff but not crumbly. Add a bit of milk if it's too stiff, a bit more flour if too moist.

3. Pinch off dough and roll with floured hands into little snakes just less than the width of a pencil. Pinch into 1" sections and toss with flour so they don't stick together. Set aside. Repeat until dough is gone. Kids love this part—let them help! Rivles do NOT have to be perfect. In fact, odd shapes give the soup character— just shoot for about even thickness. If you're in a huge hurry, you can just make pinches and don't roll them out.

4. Turn up the stock to a boil and add the rivles a handful at a time to the bubbling broth. The flour separating them can go in too. Cover and cook at a slow rolling boil until rivles are chewy but cooked through, at least 10 minutes. Stir frequently.

5. Bone out the cooled bird and tear or chop meat into spoon-size chunks. Discard bone and fat. This is the time to remove any remaining shot as you pick the meat.

6. Turn down the stock when the rivles are done and toss meat in. Add some milk with a bit of flour whisked in. Stir and thicken over medium heat. Add the eggs if using them. This is not too thick a chowder but should have some body. Make it the way you like it.

Excellent served with cornbread and honey or just homemade bread.

PAWCLAWS' OWN CALICO CREAM VEGETABLE SOUP

2 T olive oil
3 carrots, diced
3 stalks celery, diced
1 medium onion, diced
3 medium potatoes, pared and diced
$\frac{1}{2}$ C frozen corn
$\frac{1}{2}$ C frozen peas
$\frac{1}{2}$ C frozen baby lima beans
$\frac{1}{2}$ C frozen green beans
$\frac{1}{4}$ C margarine
3 T flour
2 C skimmed milk
salt and pepper

1. Pour the olive oil into a hot sauté pan and sauté the carrots, celery, and onion just to tender.
2. Place the potatoes in a saucepan, cover with water and bring to a boil. Cook for about 10 minutes.
3. In a large (*about 8-qts*) saucepan or pot, place the remaining vegetables in just enough water to cover and bring to a boil. Cook for 3 or 4 minutes, then remove from heat and drain. Allow them to cool for a few minutes, then add them to the larger pot of vegetables.
4. Rinse the potato pan and return to heat. In this pan melt the margarine, add the flour and combine well to form a roux. Add the milk all at once and whisk to a thickened medium white sauce. Bring just to a full boil, then remove from heat and add the white sauce to the large pot.
5. Add the sautéed vegetables. Stir well. Season with salt and pepper to taste and heat through.

This soup may be served with a crusty garlic bread and a green salad.

Serves 4-6

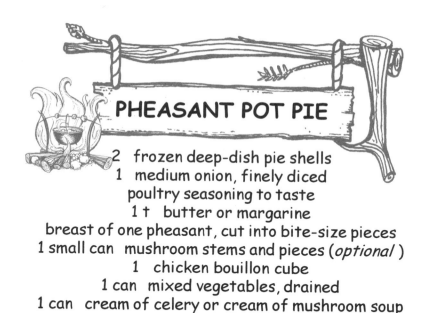

PHEASANT POT PIE

2 frozen deep-dish pie shells
1 medium onion, finely diced
poultry seasoning to taste
1 t butter or margarine
breast of one pheasant, cut into bite-size pieces
1 small can mushroom stems and pieces (*optional*)
1 chicken bouillon cube
1 can mixed vegetables, drained
1 can cream of celery or cream of mushroom soup

1. While pie crusts are thawing, sprinkle poultry seasoning on onion.
2. In skillet, melt butter. Add onion, pheasant, mushrooms and onion; sauté until pheasant is brown. Remove from heat.
3. Add mixed vegetables and soup to pheasant mixture. Pour contents of skillet into one pie crust. Use second piecrust to cover pie. Crimp edges and cut slits into top of pie.
4. Bake at 375 degrees for 50 minutes. You may want to put foil under pie to catch drippings. Serve hot.

Makes 1 pie, about 4-6 servings

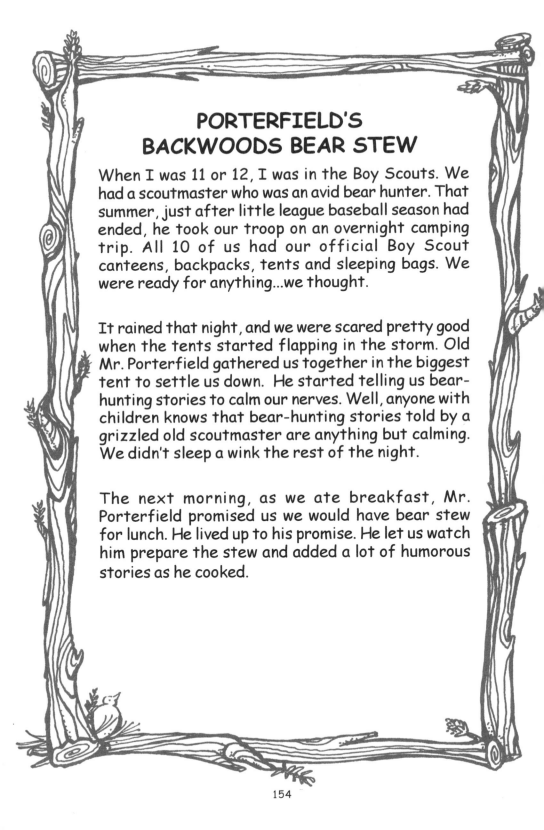

PORTERFIELD'S
BACKWOODS BEAR STEW

When I was 11 or 12, I was in the Boy Scouts. We had a scoutmaster who was an avid bear hunter. That summer, just after little league baseball season had ended, he took our troop on an overnight camping trip. All 10 of us had our official Boy Scout canteens, backpacks, tents and sleeping bags. We were ready for anything...we thought.

It rained that night, and we were scared pretty good when the tents started flapping in the storm. Old Mr. Porterfield gathered us together in the biggest tent to settle us down. He started telling us bear-hunting stories to calm our nerves. Well, anyone with children knows that bear-hunting stories told by a grizzled old scoutmaster are anything but calming. We didn't sleep a wink the rest of the night.

The next morning, as we ate breakfast, Mr. Porterfield promised us we would have bear stew for lunch. He lived up to his promise. He let us watch him prepare the stew and added a lot of humorous stories as he cooked.

PORTERFIELD'S
BACKWOODS BEAR STEW con't

2 lbs   bear meat, cut into bite-size portions
salt and pepper
2 T   flour
1 t   olive oil
water
5   celery stalks, chopped
1 lb   carrots, chopped
4   large potatoes, peeled and chopped
1   onion, diced
1 C   tomatoes
(*fresh tomatoes, canned tomatoes or tomato soup*)
1 T   Worcestershire sauce
1 t   soy sauce

1. Dredge bear meat in salt and pepper, and coat with flour.

2. Heat olive oil in a big skillet. Brown bear meat.

3. Place meat in large pot and cover with water. Boil, then reduce heat and simmer covered for 2 hours.

4. Add vegetables except tomatoes and simmer 1 hour, adding more water as needed. Add tomatoes or soup, Worcestershire sauce, soy sauce and salt and pepper to taste. Simmer 15 minutes.

5. Remove stew from heat and let sit for about 20 minutes before serving.

Serves 6-8

SNOW WHITE AND THE SEVEN BEAN CHILI

1 lb   northern beans
1 lb   mixed beans
1½-2 lbs   boneless skinless chicken breasts
2 C   chopped onions
2 T   minced garlic
2 T   olive oil
1   4-oz can chopped green chilies
2 t   ground cumin
2 t   dried oregano
¼ t   cayenne pepper (*or more to taste*)
2 t   Adobe® seasoning

1. Wash and soak beans overnight. Simmer 1½ to 2 hours until tender.
2. Bake or boil chicken breasts. Let cool a little and cut into cubes.
3. Sauté onions and garlic in olive oil. Add chilies, seasonings and chicken.
4. Add this mixture and chicken broth to beans. Simmer 30 minutes.

Serve with salsa and sour cream to taste.

Serves 4

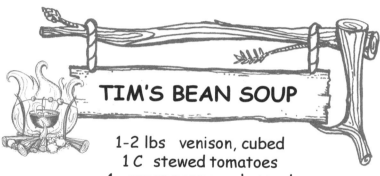

TIM'S BEAN SOUP

1-2 lbs   venison, cubed
1 C   stewed tomatoes
1   green pepper, chopped
2   jalapeno peppers, diced (*optional*)
1   onion, chopped
1   carrot, chopped
1   stalk celery, chopped
1   can black-eyed peas
2   cans kidney beans
1   can frijoles negros (*Mexican black beans*)
1   can navy beans
1   can pinto beans
$1\frac{1}{2}$ T   chili powder
salt and pepper to taste
shredded cheddar or mozzarella cheese (*optional*)

1. Place the venison, stewed tomatoes, peppers, onions, carrots and celery in a $3\frac{1}{2}$-qt or larger slow cooker.
2. Add as many of the cans of beans as you can to the cooker. When you are done you should have less than $\frac{1}{4}$" of space left in the slow cooker.
3. Add the chili powder and salt and pepper to taste. Stir all of the ingredients together.
4. Cook on high for 4 hours, or on high for 1 hour and on low for 6 hours. Best to cook it on high at least 2 hours to make sure the meat is cooked.
5. Garnish with shredded cheddar or mozzarella cheese just before serving.

Serves 6

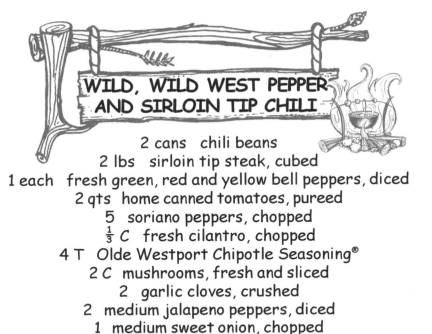

WILD, WILD WEST PEPPER AND SIRLOIN TIP CHILI

2 cans   chili beans
2 lbs   sirloin tip steak, cubed
1 each   fresh green, red and yellow bell peppers, diced
2 qts   home canned tomatoes, pureed
5   soriano peppers, chopped
$\frac{1}{3}$ C   fresh cilantro, chopped
4 T   Olde Westport Chipotle Seasoning®
2 C   mushrooms, fresh and sliced
2   garlic cloves, crushed
2   medium jalapeno peppers, diced
1   medium sweet onion, chopped
1 T   cumin
4   ancho chilis, diced
1 t   dried oregano
1 T   paprika
$\frac{1}{4}$ t   cracked black pepper
$\frac{1}{2}$ t   salt

1. Grill steak until done (*this provides a western flavor*).

2. Combine all ingredients, except mushrooms, in a crockpot and cook on low heat for 5 to 6 hours.

3. Add mushrooms and cook on high for one additional hour.

Serve with cheddar cheese, sour cream, black olives, and French bread.

VENISON CHILI

3 lbs   venison burger
1 lb   ground sausage
1 t   chili powder
2-3   cloves garlic
1 t   black pepper
½ t   white pepper
¼ t   ground cumin
2 cans   Chili Magic®
2 cans   pinto beans
1 can   kidney beans
1 can   black beans (*optional*)
3   pts tomatoes (*home canned*) or 3 cans stewed tomatoes
1 can   diced tomatoes
1 can   diced green chilies
2 cans   tomato paste with roasted garlic
1   large onion, chopped
1   large bell pepper, chopped
1 t   chili powder
½ t   ground chipotle pepper
½ t   dried oregano
¼ t   dried thyme
¼ t   dried marjoram
½ t   dried basil

Optional garnishes: shredded cheddar cheese, sour cream, sliced black olives

1. Mix first 7 ingredients in frying pan and sauté until browned. Drain off fat.

2. In a large Dutch oven or stew pot combine remaining ingredients.

3. Bring to a boil. Stir in browned meat. Turn down to low heat and simmer. Add additional seasonings to taste.

4. Top with shredded cheddar cheese, sour cream and sliced black olives.

Serves 6

CRUSTLESS
CHICKEN POT PIE

5 C   chicken broth
4 C   chicken
10 lg   celery ribs, including tops, cut into large pieces
1 C   sliced carrots
1 C   cubed potatoes
8 oz   onions, chopped
6 T   margarine
6 T   flour
$\frac{1}{2}$ t   ground white pepper
8 drops   Tabasco® sauce

1. Cook chicken and celery in 5 C chicken broth for 1 hour. Throw celery away and set chicken aside.

2. Cover carrots with water in saucepan and simmer 5 minutes or until tender. Drain and set aside.

3. Put potatoes in saucepan and just cover with water. Simmer 10 minutes.

4. Fry onion in margarine until wilted.

5. Stir flour and onion mix into 4 C heated chicken stock. Mix well. Add remaining heated stock, stirring or whisking constantly. When mixture is smooth, let it simmer for a minute then add salt, pepper and Tabasco. Layer chicken, carrots and gravy.

Bake 45 minutes at 350 degrees.

If you would love crust, put sauce in round individual dish and smash ready made biscuit on top. Cook at suggested time and temp on biscuit box then add 5 more minutes (*or they'll be too doughy*).

SIDE DISHES

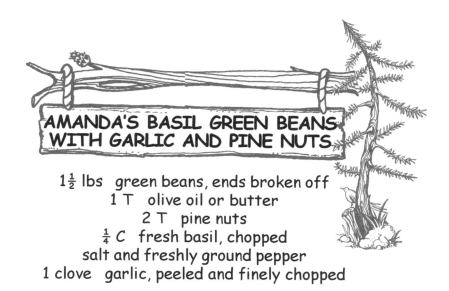

AMANDA'S BASIL GREEN BEANS WITH GARLIC AND PINE NUTS

$1\frac{1}{2}$ lbs   green beans, ends broken off
1 T   olive oil or butter
2 T   pine nuts
$\frac{1}{4}$ C   fresh basil, chopped
salt and freshly ground pepper
1 clove   garlic, peeled and finely chopped

1. Add beans to boiling pot of water and cook 5-7 minutes.
2. Remove beans from hot water and quickly rinse with cold water to stop cooking and set color. Drain.
3. In large skillet, heat olive oil. Add pine nuts and carefully toast 2-3 minutes. Remove pine nuts and set aside.
4. Add garlic to skillet and cook until soft, 1-2 minutes.
5. Add drained beans to the hot skillet and stir in the pine nuts and basil. Toss over heat until heated through. Season to taste with salt and pepper.

Serves 4-6

MOMOW'S
CORN & BROCCOLI BAKE

1   15-oz can whole kernel corn, drained
1   14-oz can cream-style corn
½ C   melted butter
1   8-oz package
Chicken-in-a-Biskit® crackers, crushed
1   10-oz package
frozen chopped broccoli, thawed

1. Combine melted butter and cracker crumbs. Reserve ½ cup crumbs for topping.
2. Mix remaining cracker crumbs, broccoli and both cans of corn. Pour into a baking dish.
3. Top with reserved cracker crumbs.
4. Bake uncovered at 375 degrees for 25-30 minutes or until lightly browned.

Serves 6-8

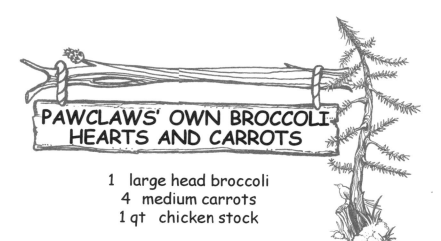

PAWCLAWS' OWN BROCCOLI HEARTS AND CARROTS

1   large head broccoli
4   medium carrots
1 qt   chicken stock

1. Remove the florets from the broccoli and store for use another day.

2. Peel the stocks, removing the tough thick fibrous skin. Slice the stalks into $\frac{1}{8}$" thick slices on the bias.

3. Pare the carrots and slice them the same way. Place in a 2-qt saucepan and cover with chicken stock by a couple of inches. Bring to a boil, reduce to a slow simmer, cover, and simmer until tender or about 15 minutes. Salt and pepper to taste before serving.

Variation: Substitute beef stock for chicken stock and add 1 tablespoon of sweet pickle relish after cooking for about 10 minutes, or two-thirds through the cooking time.

Serves 4-6

PAWCLAWS' WARM
WEATHER GREEN SALAD

1 whole clove elephant garlic, peeled
1 T coarse sea salt
½ head red lettuce, hand shredded
½ head iceberg lettuce, hand shredded
1 medium Vidalia onion, thinly sliced into rings
1 small green pepper, sliced into thin rings
1 4" piece of 1½"-diameter daikon, pared and cut into 2" thin
julienne strips.
1 medium cucumber, pared, seeds removed,
halved and cut into thin slices
1 small can of mandarin orange slices, drained
Italian salad dressing of your choice

1. Using a wooden salad bowl, rub the elephant garlic into the bottom and sides of the bowl until the oils are extracted from the garlic and it begins to turn to pulp.

2. Hand rub the sea salt into the bowl covering as much of the bowl as possible. Rap the bowl sharply with your closed hand and discard the loose contents.

3. Place the remaining ingredients into the bowl and toss well.

Serve with sufficient dressing to coat, not drown, the salad. Be sure to shake the dressing vigorously before service. Croutons, breadsticks, fresh herbs and spices may be served on the side.

This works well on really hot days with a good homemade soup or sandwich. To keep fresh and crisp outdoors toss with 5 or 6 ice cubes, place in tightly sealed plastic container and store in cooler.

Serves 4-6

ZESTY CORN ON THE COB

fresh corn ears
Old Bay® seasoning
butter
black pepper
Italian salad dressing

1. Wrap each ear of corn in a sheet of aluminum foil.
2. Add Old Bay seasoning, a slice of butter, a dash of pepper and a bit of the salad dressing.
3. Wrap tightly and cook in smoker or on grill.

Note: No added salt necessary.

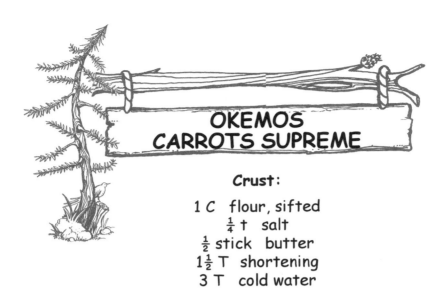

OKEMOS CARROTS SUPREME

Crust:

1 C   flour, sifted
¼ t   salt
½ stick   butter
1½ T   shortening
3 T   cold water

1. Sift together flour and salt in mixing bowl.

2. Add butter and shortening; cut in and add water quickly, tossing.

3. Press into ball. Wrap; chill dough for ½ hour or more.

4. Roll dough into ⅛" thick circle 2" larger than pie tin.

5. Line tin with chilled pastry dough. Press firmly, trim, and prick in several places with a fork to avoid bubbles.

6. Bake in hot oven at 425 degrees until crust is golden, about 8-12 minutes. Remove paper and rice and return to oven for a few minutes.

OKEMOS
CARROTS SUPREME con't

Filling:

$1\frac{3}{4}$ lbs   new carrots
$\frac{1}{2}$ C   sugar
1 C   butter
salt and pepper
$\frac{1}{2}$ C   heavy cream

1. Peel and wash carrots and cut into thin slices.
2. Cook $\frac{1}{2}$ C carrots in boiling salted water until tender.
3. Stew remaining carrots in a little water with a pinch of salt and pepper, the sugar and half the butter. When tender, juice should be completely reduced.
4. Puree carrots and add remaining butter bit by bit. Add cream, mix, reheat and pour into baked pastry shell.
5. Decorate with the slices of cooked carrots.
6. Sprinkle with a little sugar and bake at 425 degrees for 20 minutes.

Makes 1 pie

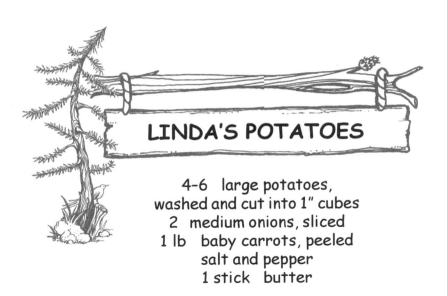

LINDA'S POTATOES

4-6 large potatoes,
washed and cut into 1" cubes
2 medium onions, sliced
1 lb baby carrots, peeled
salt and pepper
1 stick butter

1. In a 3-qt casserole dish (*coated with no-stick spray*), layer potatoes, carrots and onion slices. Salt and pepper to taste.

2. Cube butter on top.

3. Cover and bake at 400 degrees for about 1 hour, or until potatoes are done.

Serves 6-8

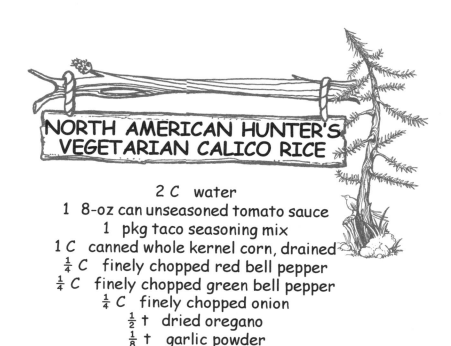

NORTH AMERICAN HUNTER'S VEGETARIAN CALICO RICE

2 C   water
1   8-oz can unseasoned tomato sauce
1   pkg taco seasoning mix
1 C   canned whole kernel corn, drained
$\frac{1}{4}$ C   finely chopped red bell pepper
$\frac{1}{4}$ C   finely chopped green bell pepper
$\frac{1}{4}$ C   finely chopped onion
$\frac{1}{2}$ t   dried oregano
$\frac{1}{8}$ t   garlic powder
1 C   uncooked brown rice

1. In a medium saucepan, combine all ingredients except rice. Bring mixture to a boil over medium heat.

2. Stir in rice. Return to a boil. Stir, then reduce heat to low; cover and weight the lid. Simmer for 20 minutes.

3. Remove from heat but do not remove lid. Set aside still covered, for 35 minutes.

4. Fluff with a fork before serving with soy sauce or salsa of your choice.

Serves 2-4

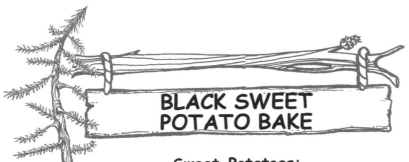

BLACK SWEET POTATO BAKE

Sweet Potatoes:

1 28-oz can sweet potatoes, drained
2 medium bananas
½ C orange juice
½ C dark brown sugar
¼ C half-and-half or light cream
¼ C pure maple syrup
3 T ground cinnamon
2 T butter or margarine
1 T five-spice powder
1 T ground ginger

1. Preheat the oven to 300 degrees.
2. Combine all ingredients at a slow speed in a blender or with a mixer until about the consistency of a firm applesauce.
3. Pour the mixture into an oven-safe dish.
4. Prepare the topping.

BLACK SWEET
POTATO BAKE con't

Topping:

¼ lb   butter
1 T   salt
½ lb   fancy pecan halves
2 T   dark brown sugar

1. Melt the butter and dissolve the salt over medium heat.
2. Add the pecans and stir until well coated and they begin to toast.
3. Spread the pecans on paper towels to drain and dry.
4. Smooth the potato mixture with a spatula and arrange the pecans on top in an artistic pattern of circular rows. Sprinkle the brown sugar over the pecans as evenly as possible.
5. Bake uncovered at 300 degrees for 20 minutes or until the sugar is completely dissolved.

Makes 1 pie, serves 6-8

OLD-FASHIONED APPLE BUTTER

13 apples,
preferably Jonathan or Winesap
2 C apple juice
sugar
cinnamon
allspice
cloves
$\frac{1}{2}$ C sauterne wine (*optional*)

1. Wash, core and quarter apples (*do not peel*).
2. Combine apples and apple juice in lightly oiled crockpot. Cover and cook on low for 10-18 hours or on high for 2-4 hours.
3. When fruit is tender, put through food mill to remove peels.
4. Measure cooked fruit and return to crockpot. For each pint of sieved cooked fruit, add 1 C sugar, 1 t cinnamon, $\frac{1}{2}$ t allspice, and $\frac{1}{2}$ t cloves.
5. Stir well, cover and cook on high setting for 6-8 hours, stirring about every 2 hours.
6. Remove cover after 3 hours to allow fruit and juice to cook down. Add wine during the last hour of cooking.
7. Spoon into hot sterilized jars and process in boiling water bath; seal.

Makes 5 $\frac{1}{2}$-pint jars

DEERCAMP DAN'S TATERS

1 small onion, sliced
1 small bell pepper, sliced
5-6 strips of bacon, cut in half
1 t oil
6-8 potatoes, sliced like french fries
1 T lemon pepper
salt
pepper

1. Heat a nonstick skillet. Sauté onions, bell peppers and bacon in oil until onions are transparent.
2. Add potatoes and fry until desired crispness is reached. Stir often.
3. Add lemon pepper, and salt and pepper to taste.
4. Drain well on paper towel.

Serves 5-6

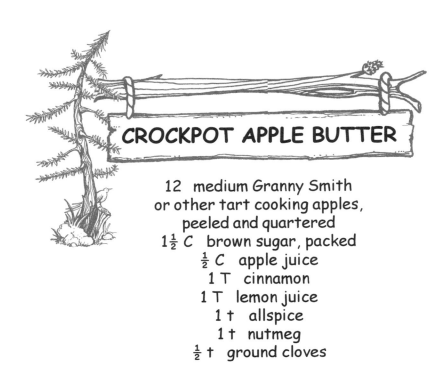

CROCKPOT APPLE BUTTER

12 medium Granny Smith
or other tart cooking apples,
peeled and quartered
1½ C brown sugar, packed
½ C apple juice
1 T cinnamon
1 T lemon juice
1 t allspice
1 t nutmeg
½ t ground cloves

1. Mix all ingredients in a large crockpot.

2. Cook 8-10 hours on low, covered. Stir.

3. Cook an additional 1-2 hours uncovered.

Makes about 3 pints

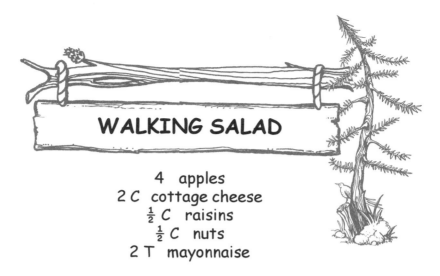

WALKING SALAD

4   apples
2 C cottage cheese
½ C raisins
½ C nuts
2 T mayonnaise

1. Cut the tops off the apples and core them, leaving the skin intact.
2. Scoop out the inside of the apples and chop this with cottage cheese, raisins and nuts. Mix with mayonnaise.
3. Stuff the mix back into the apples and put the top back on the apple.

This is a good one for taking into the duck blind.

Serves 4

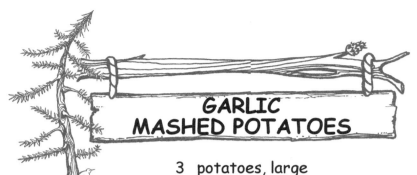

GARLIC
MASHED POTATOES

3   potatoes, large
1 T   fresh garlic, minced
½ lb   butter
½ C   Parmesan cheese, freshly grated
half and half
salt and pepper to taste
1 t   tumeric
beet juice (*optional*)

1. Cook potatoes until tender. Add all ingredients at once but don't overbeat.
2. Add tumeric at beginning then add more for deeper color. If you want pink, use beet juice instead of tumeric.

Serves 4

SMOKED MICHIGAN WHITEFISH MOUSSE

1 C   onion, chopped
8 oz   unsalted butter
1 lb smoked whitefish, cleaned, defatted
8 oz   cream cheese, room temperature
juice of ½ lemon
white and cayenne pepper
fresh dill

1. Sauté onion slowly in butter, until transparent. Cool to room temperature.
2. Process in food processor along with whitefish, cream cheese, lemon juice and peppers.
3. When mixture is smooth and fluffy, turn into individual ramekins, chill and garnish with fresh dill.

Makes about 3 cups

Wonderful and wonderfully easy. Chef notes that mixture may be piped into small gougere (*cream puffs*) or served as is for an hors d'oeuvre. After processing, the mixture can be put through a fine sieve for a smoother mousse.

Harlan W. Peterson
Tapawingo

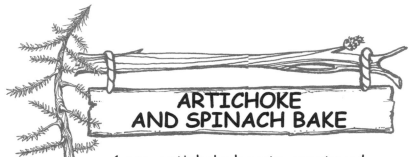

ARTICHOKE AND SPINACH BAKE

1 can   artichoke hearts, quartered
1 lg can   spinach
5 T   olive oil
1   medium onion
5 eggs, slightly beaten
1½ C   dry Monterey cheese, grated
2   cloves garlic, sliced very thin
2 T   parsley
1 t   savory
½ t   thyme
salt and pepper

1. Drain spinach. Chop fine in chopping bowl with onion, garlic, parsley and herbs.

2. Add eggs, olive oil, cheese, artichokes. Mix well and season with salt and pepper.

3. Place in oiled square 9" x 9" square baking pan.
   Bake 20 minutes at 350 degrees.

4. Cut into squares

Serves 4

CHESTNUT
STUFFING FOR GOOSE

½ T onion, chopped finely
3 T butter
¼ lb salt pork, finely chopped
½ c fresh mushrooms, finely chopped
1 C chestnut puree
⅓ C stale bread crumbs
½ T parsley, finely chopped
24 chestnuts, cooked and added whole

1. Cook onions in butter.
2. Add sausage and cook.
3. Add mushrooms, puree, parsley, salt and pepper and bring to boil.
4. Add bread crumbs and stir in chestnuts.
5. Bake at 350 degrees for 30 minutes.

Serves 4

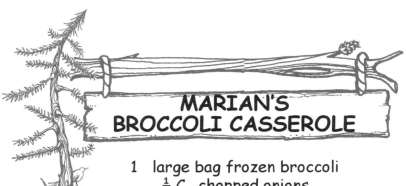

MARIAN'S BROCCOLI CASSEROLE

1   large bag frozen broccoli
½ C   chopped onions
1   stalk of celery, chopped
1 C   grated cheese
1   can cream of mushroom soup
salt and pepper
1 stick   margarine
1   box Ritz® crackers, crushed

1. Cook broccoli according to directions.
2. In large bowl, mix cooked broccoli, onion, celery, cheese and mushroom soup. Salt and pepper to taste.
3. Pour into casserole dish.
4. For topping melt margarine and add to crushed crackers in a bowl. Pour on top of casserole.
5. Bake at 350 degrees for 45 minutes.

Serves 2-4

CAMP SITE
FRUIT ICE CREAM

1 gallon   Ziploc® bag
1 quart   Ziploc® bag
2 C   half and half
¼ C   canned pie filling, any fruit flavor
1½ t   granulated sugar or sugar substitute (Equal®)
⅔ lb   ice
¼ C   rock salt

1. Combine all ingredients except the ice and rock salt into the 1-qt bag. Zip closed and combine well by squeezing and shaking. (*May be stirred before closing.*)

2. Place the sealed bag inside the gallon-size bag. Add the ice and rock salt to the gallon-size bag and distribute around the smaller bag more or less equally.

3. Seal the outer bag and shake/agitate until the cream is thickened to the desired consistency. This may take up to a half hour depending on your shaking fury and consistency preferences.

4. Additional ice and rock salt may be added as the ice melts.

The same method may be used to freeze juice pops and pudding pops purchased in the unfrozen state.

Makes about 1 pint

BILL THE ROGUE'S BLACK FOREST PIE

Crust:

1⅓ C chocolate snap cookie crumbs or chocolate graham cracker crumbs (*use food processor or blender*)
½ C ground almonds, ground in food processor or blender
½ C sugar
½ C melted butter or margarine

1. Mix dry crust ingredients together well, and then add the melted margarine. Work ingredients with fork or pastry blender until well blended.
2. Press crust onto bottom and sides of two deep 9" pie plates or tins. A glass measuring cup or coffee mug with sloping sides makes an excellent tool for this job.

Chocolate Mousse Filling:

16 oz semi-sweet chocolate
6 T powdered sugar
6 T strong brewed coffee
4-6 egg yolks
1¼ C prepared whipped topping

1. Melt chocolate in double boiler. Don't let the water boil when melting chocolate or it will scorch!
2. Add sugar, coffee, and egg yolks, one at a time. Stir until mixture has thickened. Remove from heat. Beat with mixer or wire whip until silky smooth. Allow to cool.
3. Fold in the prepared whipped topping.
4. Spoon mousse into pie crusts, filling about ½ to ⅔ full. Place in refrigerator to chill.

BILL THE ROGUE'S
BLACK FOREST PIE con't

Topping:

$1\frac{1}{4}$ C whipped topping
1 can cherry pie filling
sliced almonds for garnish
shaved semi-sweet chocolate
green sugar crystals for garnish

1. Smooth whipped topping onto top of chilled pies, leaving a bit of a depression in the middle for the cherry filling. Place in the freezer to partially freeze, about $\frac{1}{2}$ hour.

2. Carefully spoon cherry pie filling into middle of depression left in the whipped topping. Allow about an inch of the whipped topping to show all the way around.

3. Garnish using the sliced almonds to make floral shapes - the green sugar crystals for leaves and stems, and the shaved semi-sweet chocolate for the garden soil. Also sprinkle chocolate shavings around the edges. Chill in the refrigerator until ready to serve.

Makes two 9" pies

MAN'S CAKE

1 C sugar
½ C shortening
2 eggs, separated
2 t baking powder
½ t salt
2¼ C flour
1 C strong coffee
1 t vanilla extract
¾ C pecans or walnuts

1. Cream sugar, shortening and egg yolks together.
   Add dry ingredients.
2. Add coffee, vanilla and nuts. Beat egg whites until stiff and
   fold into batter.
3. Pour into greased and floured Bundt or tube pan.
4. Bake 40-60 minutes at 350 degrees. Cool slightly, then
   remove from pan; cool completely. Sprinkle with powdered
   sugar when cool.

Makes 1 cake, about 8-12 servings

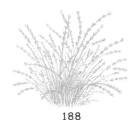

APRICOT NECTAR CAKE

1　box yellow cake mix
4　eggs
1　small package lemon gelatin
3 t　lemon extract
¾ C　canned apricot nectar
½ C　vegetable oil

1. Mix all ingredients well.
2. Pour into greased and floured Bundt pan.
3. Bake at 325 degrees for 1 hour. Turn cake onto plate and top with icing glaze.

Icing Glaze:

1¼ C　powdered sugar
¼ C　lemon juice

1. Mix together until smooth.
2. Pour over cake.

ICE CREAM IN A CAN

1 C   cream
$\frac{3}{4}$ C   whole milk
1   egg
$\frac{1}{2}$ C   sugar
1 t   vanilla extract
2   different sized cans with TIGHT lids
(*such as coffee cans*)
ice
rock salt

1. Mix cream, milk, egg, sugar and vanilla. Place in small can.

2. Place smaller can with TIGHT lid inside the larger can.

3. Put ice and rock salt around the smaller can. Put lid on larger can and roll can around for about 25 minutes, until consistency of soft ice cream.

Makes about 1 pint

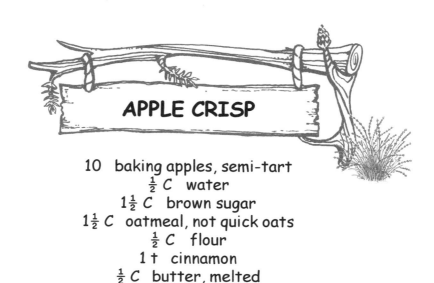

APPLE CRISP

10 baking apples, semi-tart
½ C water
1½ C brown sugar
1½ C oatmeal, not quick oats
½ C flour
1 t cinnamon
½ C butter, melted

1. Peel and core apples. Slice and arrange in 9" X 13" pan. Add water.

2. Combine dry ingredients and add butter. Stir until crumbly.

3. Spread crumbs evenly over apples.

4. Bake at 350 degrees for 40-45 minutes.

5. Serve alone or with milk or ice cream.

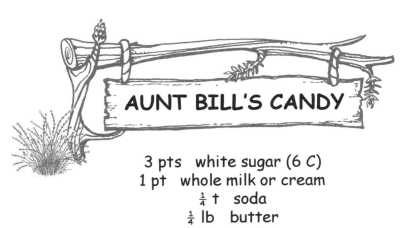

AUNT BILL'S CANDY

3 pts   white sugar (6 C)
1 pt   whole milk or cream
$\frac{1}{4}$ t   soda
$\frac{1}{4}$ lb   butter
1 t   vanilla
2 lbs   nutmeats (*pecans or walnuts*)

1. Pour 1 pt sugar into heavy iron skillet and place over low heat.
2. Begin stirring with wooden spoon and keep the sugar moving so it will not scorch. This will take about 30 minutes. Be sure not to let it smoke. It should turn light brown.
3. Meanwhile, pour remaining 2 pts of sugar and milk into deep heavy kettle; set over low heat. As soon as the other pt of sugar is melted, slowly pour it into the boiling milk and sugar, in a very fine stream.
4. Continue cooking and stirring until it forms a firm ball in cold water.
5. Take off heat, add soda and stir well. Add the butter and stir until it melts.
6. Let sit at room temperature for 10 minutes. Then add vanilla and begin beating. Use a wooden spoon and beat until thick with a dull appearance.
7. Add broken nutmeats and blend.
8. Pour into a wide, deep pan. Cut into squares when cool.

Makes about 6 lbs. Better for two to work together, as it takes much stirring and beating!!

BAKE SALE CHOCOLATE SHEET CAKE

1 stick margarine
$3\frac{1}{2}$ T cocoa
1 C water
$\frac{1}{2}$ C shortening
2 C flour
2 C sugar
1 t baking soda
$\frac{1}{3}$ C buttermilk
2 eggs, well beaten
1 t vanilla
1 t cinnamon

1. Mix first 4 ingredients in saucepan and bring to boil.
2. Remove from heat and add remaining ingredients.
3. Pour into a greased and floured 13" x 9" baking dish or edged cookie sheet.
4. Bake at 400 degrees for 30 minutes. Can be used like this for brownies or topped with the following icing.

Chocolate Icing:

1 stick margarine
3 T cocoa
$\frac{1}{3}$ C milk
$3\frac{1}{2}$ C powdered sugar
1 t vanilla
1 C chopped pecans

1. Boil first 3 ingredients in saucepan for 1 minute.
2. Remove from heat and add powdered sugar, vanilla and pecans.
3. Pour over hot cake.

EASY PEACH PIE

1 C   sugar
1 C   water
3 T   cornstarch
3 T   peach gelatin
1   prebaked pie crust
6   ripe peaches, peeled and sliced

1. Cook sugar, water, cornstarch and gelatin on medium heat until thickened. Cool.

2. Mix in peaches and put in pie crust.

3. Refrigerate until set.

Makes 1 pie

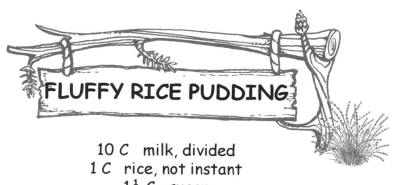

FLUFFY RICE PUDDING

10 C milk, divided
1 C rice, not instant
1¼ C sugar
1 egg
1 t vanilla extract
ground cinnamon, optional

1. Cook together 9 C milk, rice and sugar for approximately 1 hour at low to medium heat, stirring often. Cook until rice is done and starts to thicken.

2. Add reserved 1 C milk mixed with egg.

3. Pour into cooked rice mixture and cook for 1 minute more. Add vanilla.

4. Cool and sprinkle with cinnamon if desired.

Serves 4-6

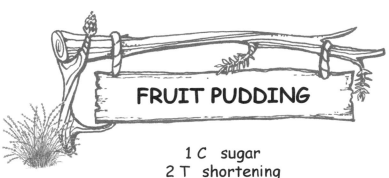

FRUIT PUDDING

1 C   sugar
2 T   shortening
2 C   flour
2 t   baking powder
1 C   milk
¾ C   sugar
1 C   hot water
2 C   fresh fruit

1. Mix 1 C sugar and shortening well.

2. In a second bowl, mix flour, baking powder and milk. Add shortening and sugar; mix well.

3. Place batter in greased and floured 13" x 9" pan.

4. Heat ¾ C sugar in 1 C hot water until dissolved. Add fresh fruit to sugar mixture.

5. Pour fruit and sugar mixture over top of batter.

6. Bake at 375 degrees for 40 minutes. The cake batter will rise to the top while baking.

If using canned fruit, you can use the juice from fruit instead of the 1 C of hot water and only use ½ C of sugar.

Serves 2-4

GRAM REEDER'S FILLED COOKIES

Cookie Dough:

½ C shortening
1 C sugar
1 egg
½ t vanilla extract
3 C flour
1 t baking powder
1 t baking soda
pinch of salt
½ C milk

Cream shortening and sugar. Add egg and vanilla. Combine dry ingredients and add to egg mixture alternating with milk. Roll out and cut into 3" circles.

Filling:

1 C raisins or dates (*or both*)
½ C sugar
1 C chopped nuts (*walnuts, pecans, etc.*)
½ C water
1 T flour, heaping

1. In a saucepan combine all ingredients and heat until mixture starts to bubble. Remove from heat.
2. Place dough circles on cookie sheet, spacing about 2" apart. Spoon filling in center of each circle and top with another dough circle.
3. Press edges closed and poke hole in top of cookie.
4. Bake at 350 degrees until cookie dough is done, about 10-14 minutes

Makes about 3 dozen cookies

LAVENDER ICE CREAM

2 C half-and-half
2 T fresh or dried lavender blossoms
6 large egg yolks
½ C sugar
1½ C heavy cream

1. Bring half-and-half to boil, add lavender and cook 1½ minutes.

2. Allow mixture to sit for 2 hours, until flavor has settled.

3. Pour mixture through cheesecloth to strain blossoms from mixture (*discard lavender*).

4. Heat strained mixture until hot but not boiling.

5. Beat egg yolks and sugar in bowl until pale and thickened. Slowly add a little of the half-and-half mixture to the egg yolks to cool them, then combine both mixtures in saucepan.

6. Stir gently over medium heat until the mixture coats the back of a spoon. This takes about 10 minutes. Do not let mixture boil. Stir heavy cream into custard mixture and refrigerate for 2 hours or until cold.

7. Put mixture in ice cream maker and freeze.

Makes approximately 1 qt

LOUISE'S
APPLE DAPPLE CAKE

3 eggs
1½ C vegetable oil
2 t vanilla extract
2 C sugar
1 t salt
3 C flour
1 t baking soda
3 C chopped apples
1 C chopped pecans or walnuts
1 C brown sugar
½ C butter
¼ C water

1. Beat eggs, oil, vanilla and sugar well.

2. Add dry ingredients, mixing well.

3. Fold in apples and nuts.

4. Pour into greased and floured 10" tube pan and bake at 350 degrees for 1 hour.

5. Just before removing the cake from the oven: In a small saucepan bring to a boil brown sugar, butter and water. Let boil 3 minutes.

6. Remove cake from oven and place on cooling rack. Pour glaze over hot cake while still in pan.

Makes 1 cake, about 8-12 servings

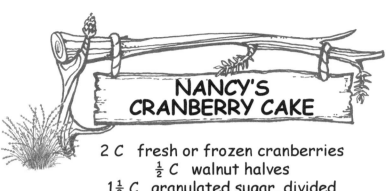

NANCY'S CRANBERRY CAKE

2 C fresh or frozen cranberries
½ C walnut halves
1½ C granulated sugar, divided
¾ C butter or margarine, softened
2 eggs, beaten
1 C flour
½ t baking powder
2 t almond extract

1. Place cranberries, walnuts, and ½ cup sugar in a bowl and stir together to coat the cranberries.
2. Put in a greased 9" cake or pie pan.
3. Cream together margarine, remaining 1 C sugar and eggs. Add dry ingredients and almond extract.
4. Spread over cranberries and bake for 1 hour at 350 degrees.

May be served warm in pie wedges or invert after removing from oven to have the top of the cake become a red glazed surface suitable for topping with whipped cream or ice cream.

Serves 6-8

NEVER-FAIL
EGG CUSTARD PIE

4 eggs, slightly beaten
$\frac{1}{2}$ C sugar
$\frac{1}{4}$ t salt
1 t vanilla extract
$2\frac{1}{2}$ C milk, scalded
1 C fresh or defrosted frozen berries of choice
1 9" frozen unbaked pie crust

1. Mix eggs, sugar, salt and vanilla.

2. Pour scalded milk over mixture.

3. Arrange your favorite berries in the bottom of the unbaked pie crust. (*if using frozen berries, drain first*).

4. Pour custard mixture over berries.

5. Bake at 425 degrees for 10 minutes; reduce heat to 375 degrees and bake until custard is firm, about 25 minutes.

6. Chill and serve.

Makes 1 pie, serves 6-8

NO-FUSS FUDGE

4 C sugar
1 stick butter, melted
½ C peanut butter
½ C cocoa
2 T milk
2 T vanilla

1. Combine all ingredients in bowl and mix until smooth and creamy.
2. Pour into ungreased shallow pan and chill in refrigerator for 2 hours.
3. Cut into cubes and serve.

OMA'S GERMAN BUTTER COOKIES

1 lb   butter
4 C   sugar
4   eggs
8 C   flour
2 t   baking powder
sugar sprinkles

1. Cream butter and sugar until creamy. Add eggs, mix well.

2. Slowly add flour and baking powder. Add a little bit of milk if necessary.

3. On floured board work dough gently. Cut dough into quarters. Roll out, a quarter at a time, to about $\frac{1}{4}$" thick. Cut out shapes with cookie cutter.

4. Place on cookie sheet and decorate with sprinkles.

5. Bake at 375 degrees for 10-15 minutes.

Note: You may not be able to mix all flour in at first, especially if using a mixer. Mix in the rest by hand as you work the dough. Dough should be soft, not stiff.

PEACHES AND CREAM CAKE

$\frac{3}{4}$ C   flour
$\frac{1}{2}$ C   milk
1   egg
$\frac{1}{2}$ t   salt
3 T   soft margarine
1   pkg vanilla pudding mix, small (*not instant*)
1 t   baking powder
1 can   sliced peaches, drained (*save the juice*)
1   8-oz package cream cheese
3 T   peach juice
$\frac{1}{2}$ C + 1 t   sugar
1 t   ground cinnamon

1. Combine flour, milk, egg, salt, margarine, pudding mix and baking powder. Mix together for 2 minutes on medium speed.
2. Pour into buttered 9" pie pan. Lay drained peaches over the batter.
3. Combine cream cheese, peach juice, and $\frac{1}{2}$ cup sugar. Beat for 2 minutes on medium speed.
4. Pour over peaches and batter.
5. Combine cinnamon and remaining 1 t sugar. Sprinkle over top.

Bake at 350 degrees for 30 to 35 minutes.

Makes 1 small cake, serves 6-8

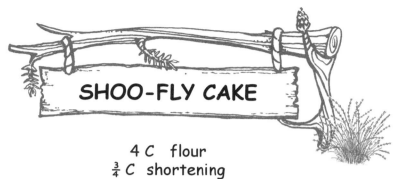

SHOO-FLY CAKE

4 C   flour
¾ C   shortening
2 C   brown sugar
2 C   boiling water
1 C   molasses
1 T   baking soda

1. Combine flour, shortening and brown sugar. Mix thoroughly.

2. Reserve 1 cup crumb mixture for topping.

3. To the remaining crumb mixture add boiling water, molasses and baking soda. Mix well and pour into greased 9" X 13" cake pan.

4. Sprinkle remaining crumbs on top.

5. Bake at 350 degrees until toothpick inserted into center comes out clean.

Serves 8-12

SWEET POTATO CUSTARD PIE

½ lb   fancy pecan halves
½   stick butter
1 T   salt
1   29-oz can cut sweet potatoes (*do not drain*)
½ C   flour
½ C   sugar
½ C   light brown sugar
2   eggs
¼ C   softened butter
2 t   vanilla extract
1 t   ground cinnamon
1 t   baking powder
½ t   salt
1   unbaked 9" deep-dish pie shell
ice cream or whipped cream (*optional*)

1. Combine the pecans, butter and salt in a heated skillet and toss until the pecan halves are well coated and most of the butter is absorbed.

2. Drain and cool the nuts on paper towels.

3. In a large mixing bowl beat the potatoes and liquid until the potatoes are softened and somewhat smooth. Add the remaining ingredients one at a time and continue beating the mixture. Whip to a very smooth consistency. A couple table spoons of half-and-half or heavy cream may be added for richness.

4. Pour the mixture into the pie shell and place in 350-degree oven for 30 minutes.

5. Remove to a working surface. Arrange the pecans on top pie.

6. Return pie to oven and continue baking until the center is firm, about 30 minutes more.

Cool and serve as a dessert pie with ice cream or whipped topping.

Makes 1 pie, about 6-8 servings

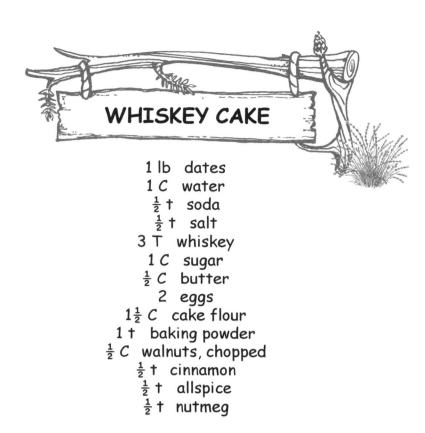

WHISKEY CAKE

1 lb dates
1 C water
½ t soda
½ t salt
3 T whiskey
1 C sugar
½ C butter
2 eggs
1½ C cake flour
1 t baking powder
½ C walnuts, chopped
½ t cinnamon
½ t allspice
½ t nutmeg

1. Boil dates in water. Cool and add soda, salt and whiskey.

2. Blend in sugar, butter, eggs, flour and baking powder.

3. Add nuts, cinnamon, allspice and nutmeg.

4. Add date mixture to sugar mixture.

5. Bake in two 8" cake pans for 30 minutes at 350 degrees, or until a knife comes out clean.

Frosting for Whiskey Cake

2 C brown sugar
14 T cream
1 t vanilla

1. Boil brown sugar and cream until it forms a soft ball.

2. Cool thoroughly then beat until stiff. Add vanilla.

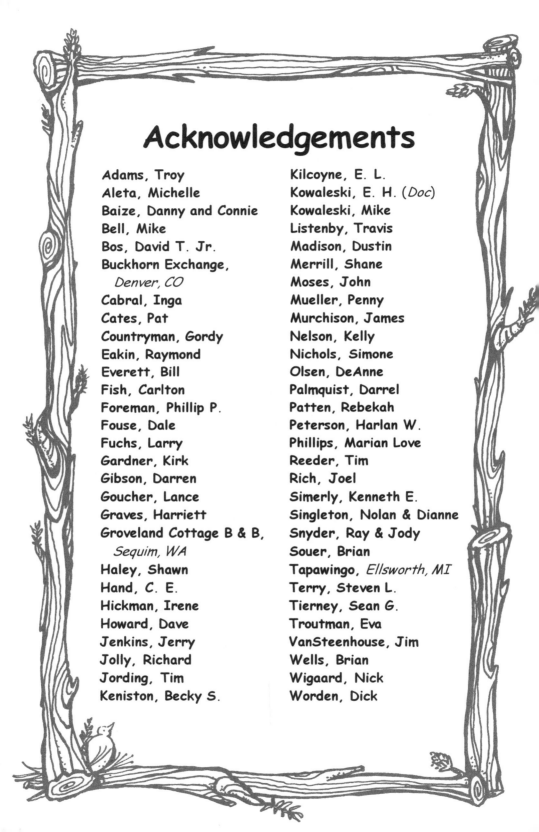

Acknowledgements

Adams, Troy
Aleta, Michelle
Baize, Danny and Connie
Bell, Mike
Bos, David T. Jr.
Buckhorn Exchange,
   Denver, CO
Cabral, Inga
Cates, Pat
Countryman, Gordy
Eakin, Raymond
Everett, Bill
Fish, Carlton
Foreman, Phillip P.
Fouse, Dale
Fuchs, Larry
Gardner, Kirk
Gibson, Darren
Goucher, Lance
Graves, Harriett
Groveland Cottage B & B,
   Sequim, WA
Haley, Shawn
Hand, C. E.
Hickman, Irene
Howard, Dave
Jenkins, Jerry
Jolly, Richard
Jording, Tim
Keniston, Becky S.

Kilcoyne, E. L.
Kowaleski, E. H. (*Doc*)
Kowaleski, Mike
Listenby, Travis
Madison, Dustin
Merrill, Shane
Moses, John
Mueller, Penny
Murchison, James
Nelson, Kelly
Nichols, Simone
Olsen, DeAnne
Palmquist, Darrel
Patten, Rebekah
Peterson, Harlan W.
Phillips, Marian Love
Reeder, Tim
Rich, Joel
Simerly, Kenneth E.
Singleton, Nolan & Dianne
Snyder, Ray & Jody
Souer, Brian
Tapawingo, *Ellsworth, MI*
Terry, Steven L.
Tierney, Sean G.
Troutman, Eva
VanSteenhouse, Jim
Wells, Brian
Wigaard, Nick
Worden, Dick

INDEX

- **TELEPHONE ORDERS** 303.751.2454
- **FAX ORDERS** 303.671.5200
- **MAIL ORDERS** **Simpler Life Press**
  1599 South Uinta Way
  Denver, Colorado 80231
- INTERNET ORDERS www.vansteenhouse.com
- EMAIL ORDERS cookbook@vansteenhouse.com

Deer Camp Dan's Cookbook $15.95

Name _____

Address _____

City _____ State _____

Zip _____ Telephone (____) _____

PAYMENT OPTIONS

Check: Please make check payable to Simpler Life Press
Paypal: https://www.paypal.com/refer/pal=andrea%40home.com

SALES TAX

Please add 2.9% for books shipped to Colorado address

SHIPPING AND HANDLING

$4.00 for the first book and $2.00 for each additional book

Total Payment _____

Call and order now!

303.751.2454

HILC IN-HOME CARE

1010 Highway 28 West
Owensville, MO 65066

573-437-5111
866-231-6652

Medicaid • Veteran's • Respite • Private Pay • Private Insurance

---

FOR All OF THOSE WHO HAVE LOST THEY'RE SIGHT,

All OF THEIR LIFE SEEMS BLACK AS NIGHT

FOR ALL OF US WHO OPEN OUR EYES

WE WILL BE SAVED IN THE LAMBS LIGHT.

YOUR MEMORY REMAINS, BUT YOU'VE BEEN
GONE SO LONG - I JUST KEEP ON LIVING,
BUT IT SEEMS SO WRONG. I MISS YOU NOW...
I MISS YOU SO MUCH... MY HEART JUST KEEPS
BREAKING, SORROWFUL PAIN, SADLY ENOUGH.

WHAT CAN I DO, WHAT CAN I SAY
I GET DOWN ON MY KNEES AND PRAY

JESUS HEARS MY PRAYERS, MY WORDS SPOKEN
AND ~~GOD~~ HAS PLANS — MUCH MORE THAN A JOKEN
— RE-PHRASE ↑

GOD HAS PLANS OF THIS I'M SURE
HIS SON CAME HERE, A A MAN SO PURE
HE PAYED FOR MY SINS — A DEBT HE DIDNT OWE
TO COVER FOR ~~OUR~~ SINS — A DEBT I DID OWE
                MY ↑
        MOVE AROUND